General Editor

David Daiches

Professor of English in the School of English
and American Studies, University of Sussex

FOR LAL
AND
TROILUS DAVID

D. H. LAWRENCE:
THE RAINBOW

by

FRANK GLOVER SMITH

*Lecturer in the School of English and American Studies,
University of Sussex*

EDWARD ARNOLD

Printed in Great Britain by
The Camelot Press Ltd, Southampton

General Preface

The object of this series is to provide studies of individual novels, plays and groups of poems and essays which are known to be widely read by students. The emphasis is on clarification and evaluation; biographical and historical facts, while they may be discussed when they throw light on particular elements in a writer's work, are generally subordinated to critical discussion. What kind of work is this? What exactly goes on here? How good is this work, and why? These are the questions that each writer will try to answer.

It should be emphasized that these studies are written on the assumption that the reader has already read carefully the work discussed. The objective is not to enable students to deliver opinions about works they have not read, nor is it to provide ready-made ideas to be applied to works that have been read. In one sense all critical interpretation can be regarded as foisting opinions on readers, but to accept this is to deny the advantages of any sort of critical discussion directed at students or indeed at anybody else. The aim of these studies is to provide what Coleridge called in another context 'aids to reflection' about the works discussed. The interpretations are offered as suggestive rather than as definitive, in the hope of stimulating the reader into developing further his own insights. This is after all the function of all critical discourse among sensible people.

DAVID DAICHES

Contents

NOTE ON THE TEXT

Page numerals for quotations from *The Rainbow* refer to the text used throughout: Phoenix Edition, Heinemann, 1963.

OTHER WORKS—ABBREVIATED REFERENCES AND EDITIONS

AP   'A Propos of Lady Chatterley's Lover' in *Sex, Literature and Censorship*, ed. H. T. Moore, Twayne, 1953

Apoc.   *Apocalypse* (1931), Secker, 1932

C.P.   *Complete Poems*, 2 vols., ed. V. de Sola Pinto and W. Roberts, Heinemann, 1964; revised, 1967

Fant.   *Fantasia of the Unconscious* (1923), Phoenix edn., Heinemann, 1961

L.I, L.II   *Collected Letters*, Vols. I and II, ed. H. T. Moore, Viking Press, 1962

P. & U.   *Psychoanalysis and the Unconscious* (1923), Phoenix edn., Heinemann, 1961

PX I   *Phoenix Posthumous Papers of D. H. Lawrence*, ed. E. D. McDonald, Heinemann, 1936

PX II   *Phoenix II, Uncollected, unpublished and other prose works by D. H. Lawrence*, ed. W. Roberts and H. T. Moore, Heinemann, 1968

S.C.A.L.   *Studies in Classic American Literature* (1923), Doubleday Anchor, 1955

Also:

A.V.   *Ann Veronica*, H. G. Wells (1909), Essex edn., Benn, 1927

A.F.T.   *Anna of the Five Towns*, Arnold Bennett (1902), Penguin, 1936 and 1954

1 Marsh Farm: The Brangwens

The opening seems a key to the novel's length: family history, from this genealogy of the Brangwens, seems likely to plump out the five hundred pages. Such a beginning signals ambitious planning, a wide range of social coverage. *Middlemarch* (1873) is the obvious exemplar; more recently, *The Man of Property* (1906) had inaugurated Galsworthy's *Forsyte Saga*. Arnold Bennett followed with *The Old Wives' Tale* (1908), and his *Clayhanger* (1910), initiating a trilogy, added considerably to the great popularity of the mode. Lawrence had just been reading Thomas Mann's chronicle of four generations, *Buddenbrooks* (1901). For *The Rainbow* (1915), he adopted Mann's and Galsworthy's pattern of the generations, rather than the lateral panorama of a society. Yet the extended rhythms and the direction and tone of the narrative are more akin to those of George Eliot's novel. The trajectory of *Buddenbrooks* is one of downward motion, of narrowing and enclosing; the tone is that of decline, the direction is towards death. The fourth generation is caught and destroyed by its forbears. Lawrence reverses this: the narrative's trajectory is a forward, upward motion, a movement of enlargement and release, of rejection of all, within or without, that has the tang of decay or death. The fourth generation, in Ursula Brangwen, moves toward resolution of the earlier struggles. Ursula is emergent because experience shows her what to discard and what to accept in the living of her forbears.

The prologue that opens the first chapter sketches in these forbears, packing in details of the Brangwen people and places. They are blond, slow-speaking, vigorous farming stock, long settled in the north Midlands. Their presence, their essential livingness, is indicated with bold contours, blocked out in ways that recall Hardy's men, Gabriel Oak and Michael Henchard. Their womenfolk, sparely yet weightily evoked in the compressed history of 'the woman', are sharply registered beings. Cossethay, Ilkeston, the valley of the Erewash with farms and marshlands, where Derbyshire and Nottinghamshire meet—all are readily evoked, their atmosphere finely created. There is full-bodiedness in the representation of person, place, and scene, behind them an enriching pressure of inner meanings, thematic and symbolic. The world of appearances, without being fractured or distorted, is being made to manifest its significance. The opening section is rounded out by portrayal of the historical setting, a time of economic and social change, the 1840's—comparable, as a threshold to the major action, to the function of the 1830's in *Middlemarch*.

The opening sections, among the last written, are in a rich, suggestive, Biblical language, and seem to compose a country prologue to a chronicle novel:

> So the Brangwens came and went without fear of necessity, working hard because of the life that was in them, not for want of the money. Neither were they thriftless. . . . But heaven and earth was teeming around them, and how should this cease? They felt the rush of the sap in spring, they knew the wave which cannot halt, but every year throws forward the seed to begetting, and, falling back, leaves the young-born on the earth. They knew the intercourse between heaven and earth, sunshine drawn into the breast and bowels, the rain sucked up in the daytime, nakedness that comes under the wind in autumn, showing the birds' nests no longer worth hiding. Their life and interrelations were such; feeling the pulse and body of the soil, that opened to their furrow for the grain, and became smooth and supple after their ploughing, and clung to their feet with a weight that pulled like desire, lying hard and unresponsive when the crops were to be shorn away. The young corn waved and was silken, and the lustre slid along the limbs of the men who saw it. They took the udder of the cows, and the cows yielded milk and pulse against the hands of the men, the pulse of the blood of the teats of the cows beat into the pulse of the hands of the men. They mounted their horses, and held life between the grip of their knees, they harnessed their horses at the wagon and, with hand on the bridle-rings, drew the heaving of the horses after their will. (pp. 1 and 2)

The 'background' material, however, has here been made into foreground, for description has been moved into the enactment of theme. This passage particularly, and the section generally, adumbrates the rhythms and dramatic principles which animate the total action. It can be contrasted with the fine opening of George Eliot's *The Mill on the Floss* (1860). There, geography, history, the natural setting, the scene's particular associations, are all evoked in vivid detail and graphic phrases, shot through with the narrator's concern and loving memory. Moreover, the images—of millstream, river, and sea—which accumulate an emblematic and symbolic force, also relate past and present, and focus the implications of the action. In the Lawrence passage, the life of the images itself, as in poetry, is the life of the action, the carrier of the meanings and of the narrative significance. The purpose and effect are closer to, say, those of the opening of Hardy's *The Return of the Native* (1878) than to those of George Eliot's introduction. Hardy and Lawrence in this symbolic moulding of description bring to the novel some of the qualities of Elizabethan and Jacobean poetic drama.

The prologue is an 'inscaping' of the farm and village life through charged, metaphoric terms and through strong, vibrating rhythms. The language creates, as from the inside, the life of blood-intimacy: the inextricable bodily livingness of the earth and of the men. Earth, beast, and man alike are nourished by the annular, elemental forces, the prime organic energies which fashion all seasonal motions. Essentially, this is not a past society's mode of living recreated from loving memory. The perspective and the evaluation, implicit and explicit, are not of nostalgia, however controlled, as those of George Eliot (or, at least, of her narrator) more decidedly are. The rhythms, insistent, vigorous, the phrasing, bold, uncomplicated, the diction, forthright, unadorned, the verbs, active, often monosyllabic: all these contribute to create an imminent sense of a condition. The sense of a time-gap, the yearning for what is past, the golden haze of cherished recollection, are precluded by a realising act of imagination which brings this past into a physical, vibrating immediacy.

Lawrence often speaks of 'the religious and ritualistic rhythm of the year, in human life' (*AP/PX II*, p. 509), a rhythm which nourishes faith and hope, which expresses and serves an 'eternal human need of living in ritual adjustment to the cosmos in its revolutions'. The theoretical reflections, composed in 1929, conceptualise what is so brilliantly and richly dramatized in this novel. The rhythms and the imagery of this first section, and of so many other parallel sections and passages, are analogues and tropes to embody that religious and ritualistic rhythm of the year by which man witnesses his blood-tie with the cosmos. Perhaps the major trope working to embody this relation is the one comprising all the images of sexual encounter: begetting, seed, intercourse, nakedness, smooth and supple body. The whole of the long quoted passage revolves around a half-submerged metaphor of the coupling of earth and sky, the mating of human and divine, in which man takes on some of the power and function of a creative, incarnate god. Unselfconsciously, the metaphors have a sharply erotic cast, as with much of Hardy's imagery of nature. (An instance is Tess Durbeyfield's walk towards Angel's music-playing in the garden.) Sexual union in *The Rainbow* passage is metonymic for union of mankind and the cosmos. This begins to indicate the kind of significance Lawrence establishes for physical love, and indicates too the profoundly sacramental nature of sexual love in the permanent relation of marriage.

Significant points of comparison are provided by a part of *Four Quartets*, in which T. S. Eliot symbolises marriage, love, and social relation by the dance around the fire:

> Round and round the fire
>   Leaping through the flames, or joined in circles,
>   Rustically solemn or in rustic laughter
>   Lifting heavy feet in clumsy shoes,
>   Earth feet, loam feet, lifted in country mirth
>   Mirth of those long since under earth
>   Nourishing the corn. Keeping time,
>   Keeping the rhythm in their dancing
>   As in their living in the living seasons
>   The time of the seasons and the constellations
>   The time of milking and the time of harvest
>   The time of the coupling of man and woman
>   And that of beasts. Feet rising and falling.
>   Eating and drinking. Dung and death. (*East Coker*, I, 34–47)

The activity, the seasons, the weight of desire, the union of man and woman: the parallels are, superficially, close. Eliot's climactic phrase reminds man, however, of low beginnings and oppressive limits. The earthly is a clog, the body an enfeeblement, however it aspires. Lawrence, conversely, celebrates the earthly because the life in the body is in accord with life around it, in nature, in others, and in the cosmos .He saw the ancient world as religious and godless: men were in close physical oneness, and the whole cosmos was alive, felt in contact with the flesh of men. (To these ancients, Jung attributes a 'biological appreciation' of fellow-men.) Man's assurance and serenity stems from his responsive sense of a tremendous living flood which carries and sustains him: 'Creation is a great flood, forever flowing in lovely and terrible waves'. Man is a religious animal in maintaining himself in true connection with his contiguous universe, the myriad things he moves with, amongst, and against: 'Each thing . . . streams in its own odd, intertwining flux' (*Art and Morality*/PX I, p. 525). Heraclitus, whose words provide cryptic epigraphs for *Four Quartets*, is also present in the novelist's sense of the universe as 'a stream of all things slowly moving'.

The ancient world, men in vital relation to the circumambient universe; the English country world at the close of the eighteenth century, the Brangwens immersed in their life of blood-intimacy. The two worlds and their terms are surely interchangeable. These early Brangwens, 'facing inwards to the teeming life of creation', are patriarchal, tribal, pagan, 'staring into the sun'. They are the flesh and blood that nourish the vitality of Ursula's later quest for the titan Sons of God, authenticating her sense of the vital truth and necessity of that legend. Consider the Alfred Brangwen of the 1840's, the time of impending change: 'He was spoilt like a lord of creation.' This modern Adam is a humorous patriarch who follows his natural inclinations, falling into 'a deep tense fury' for days under his wife's sharp taunts. He is independent, she is odd and apart: 'They were two very separate beings, vitally connected, knowing nothing of each other, yet living in their separate ways from one root'. This is incisive and convincing, brief yet suggestive. One of its dramatic functions is to anticipate the comprehensive presentation of Tom Brangwen's marriage with Lydia Lensky. Yet, far from establishing a norm, its comparative role, without denigrating this earlier pair, is to sharpen our sense of the difficult, later achievements in marriage.

The Brangwens and their marriages, however, are not put before us in the form of case-histories, nor as socially typical. They exist, not in the realm of cultural allegory or of the debate of social ideals, but in the realm of mythic being: 'Myth is never an argument, it never has a didactic or moral purpose, you can draw no conclusion from it' (*PX I*, p. 296). The *Study of Thomas Hardy* offers terminology to help consider in what sense *The Rainbow* moves in the mode of myth (*PX I*, pp. 398–516). The mythic principle hypostatised in the Brangwen men is that of Law, a 'physical morality' shaped by the Jewish sense of God the Father. Creation is apprehended as one, life is pure being, man living in complete unity with all created things. His existence is in sensation, an existence in nature and in the flesh. Earth is the great source of Law, and the divinity of bodily existence has its roots in an originating central darkness. The complementary force of Love, a non-physical morality, is hypostatised in the Brangwen women. Life is apprehended as knowing, a perception of whatever is beyond the rejected self and its identity in the senses. This principle is attributed to the Christian sense of God the Son. Life is served by submission to other selves, since Love is the force of differentiation, individuation.

These universal forces and rhythms of nature are not in equilibrium, not in alternation, not in conflict. As the crown represents, not victory for either, but the life-engendering struggle between Lion and Unicorn, so God the Holy Spirit, God the Comforter, is a third term for the creative dialectic between Law and Love, Female and Male, God the Father and God the Son. In these symbolic terms, we can see that the early Brangwen men are 'female', the Brangwen women are 'male'. Like the images of dark and light, the terms are non-evaluative, free of ethical or normative formulas. They are not inferred from the novel, but the vision behind the novel's action is homologous to the vision of the *Study* and of *The Crown* (PX II, pp. 365–415). They help to stress an understanding of the nature of being, personal, social, cosmic, which is religious in kind. The action has more profound inflections than can be suggested by themes of man versus woman, adventure versus security, or the collision of two cultures.

The Brangwen women, striving for knowledge and for differentiation, turn from the way of blood-intimacy. They look to education, experience, entry into a 'finer, more vivid circle of life'. Mrs. Morel in *Sons and Lovers*, sharing such expectations, also sees in social success a compensation for the degradation of the life at home. The city looked to by the Brangwen women, however, is evoked in Prayer Book phrases, a land 'where secrets were made known and desires fullfilled'. From an enclosed way of life, they look out towards a community of fulfilment. That the 'active scope of man' brings canal, new collieries, and the railway, fashioning its versions of Wiggiston, is a complicated, bitter irony. Even the farmers, becoming suppliers and tradesmen, are roused to 'fearsome pleasure' at the new throbbings of life.

Tom Brangwen emerges as the central figure in this phase of renewal. The immediate thrust is from the Brangwen women, through his close relation to his mother. Tom distills into his nature all the qualities and potentialities of his family. Though he is the stay-at-home, inheriting Marsh Farm almost by default, he outpaces his brothers, who variously reject the older mode of living. Life is sustained by relations and by feeling-patterns which can wither away, so that there must be replacement: 'Because when these feeling-patterns become inadequate, when they will no longer body forth the workings of the yeasty soul, then we are in torture' (PX I, p. 753). Tom's yeasty nature is fermented, first by his mother's insistent affection, then by the pressures of education:

> In feeling he was developed, sensitive to the atmosphere around him,
> brutal perhaps, but at the same time delicate, very delicate. So he had a
> low opinion of himself. . . . But at the same time his feelings were
> more discriminating than those of most of the boys, and he was
> confused. He was more sensuously developed, more refined in instinct
> than they. (p. 10)

Paradoxes of temperament and of spirit are recorded here, and they
contribute forcefully to Tom Brangwen's quest for renewal.

Tom is the first of a series of child and adolescent studies in the novel,
remarkable for their verve, wit, and insight, certainly comparable to
George Eliot's. Emotional closeness to the parent electrically conducts
impulses, needs, and demands. Comparison with the representations of
this kind in *Sons and Lovers* shows the mastery now freed of any direct
involvement of the writer's own feelings. The mother leans upon Tom,
making him feel 'guilty of his own nature'. The twists and turns are
followed through schooling and boyish affection; through adolescence
and young manhood on the farm. Tom's drunkenness and vulgarity,
like his brother Frank's, are a debased form of the life of blood-intimacy,
but equally an incoherent protest at the paucity of choices available. The
impersonal and distressing initiation into sexual experience, with a
prostitute, is followed by a very different sexual relationship, with the
girl at Matlock. As he begins to feel that passion and love is a serious,
even a terrifying matter, he also responds to its delight and graciousness.
In all this, Tom Brangwen represents a version of Jude Fawley; earlier,
in *The White Peacock* (1911), George Saxton's agonising dilemmas
restated those of Hardy's hero. Tom is like Jude insofar as social changes
impinge upon his choices, and insofar as the paramount experiences of
living centre around the relation to woman.

Tom's quest for a new mode of living, for a feeling-pattern that will
let him live from his own independent centre, takes its key from the
Matlock encounters. In the girl and her aristocratic escort he sees
graciousness, delight, freedom, otherness. In his restless searching he
finds all these again, blended in the strangely disturbing Polish woman, a
housekeeper at the vicarage. Lydia Lensky is from that 'far-off world of
cities and governments and the active scope of man', yet so utterly
different from the Brangwen women who longed for that fine, vivid
existence. With a shock of recognition he cries, 'That's her!', baffled and
fascinated by her foreignness, her complete otherness. She is profoundly

withdrawn, yet passionate with a force that shows Tom how unformed all his own feelings are. Marriage begins the creative, turbulent struggle to form his feelings, in a passional connection that changes for him everything within and without:

> When it has struck home to her, like a death, 'this is *him*!'
> she has no part in it, no part whatever,
> it is the terrible *other*,
> when she knows the fearful *other flesh*. . . .
>
> I shall be cleared, distinct, single as if burnished in silver,
>
> two of us, unutterably distinguished, and in unutterable conjunction.
> (*Manifesto*, *C.P. I*, p. 262)

It takes the major part of the section to show how the fulfilment of this marriage differs so completely from the common domesticity and uxoriousness of the brother Frank, and from the restless, snobbish sexuality of the brother Alfred. Lydia and Tom's passional relation renews the instinctive bonds with the life around, restores the vigorous pulse-beat of the inherited life-mode at Marsh Farm.

The morality of relationship, of the selfhood created in passional connection, is given human lineaments in the courtship and marriage of Tom and Lydia. The novelist's compulsion to focus the action in just this way changed an attempt at a popular mode into 'an earnest and painful work':

> I can only write what I feel pretty strongly about: and that, at present, is the relation between men and women. After all, it is *the* problem of today, the establishment of a new relation, or the readjustment of the old one, between men and women. (*L.I*, p. 200)

On the page, in particular scenes, in the development of this relation, there is yet no impression of illustration of a thesis by the action. The concept of 'polarity', for example, is certainly behind the scene of Tom's visit to the vicarage (pp. 36–44). Yet it comes movingly to life in profoundly human particularity. Incidental naturalistic detail sharply, delicately, gives form to the setting: a March night, the great wind, the man in darkness looking upon the woman and girl in the lighted kitchen. Simple exchanges, gesture and talk disclose the power of mutual need, and create their passionate bond. The specific details, words, objects, are redolent of human feelings and purpose. They alone convey the sense of radical adjustment and balance, of relation-in-distinction, of the intimate ties of within and without, of man and nature. Elsewhere, as in the symbolism of metamorphosis and transfiguration (p. 33), the terms carry on the transposition of Biblical terms and allusions so characteristic of the novel. Within these configurations, there is a specific concentration of meaning in the imagery of rebirth (pp. 34 and 35). Lydia's arousal is focused by the trope of Persephone's return from the underworld. The first embrace is a death of their old selves; and nourished by being sealed together 'in the darkest sleep', they grow into new selfhood and a new union.

Before Tom's advent, alone with Anna, Lydia made the girl restless, 'strained and distorted', seeming to draw her into the past. Again, the parental, intimate demand, graphically suggested. Tom, in his turn, when Lydia's childbearing seems to obliterate him, looks for support to the girl. The relation contains now, without any perversion of feeling, something of a sexual element: 'So soon they were like lovers, father and child'. Certainly the bond is more intimate than any suggested between Tom and his sons by Lydia. Tom, like the mother, appeals to Anna for sympathy and love, but of the unquestioning kind sought from a parent by a child. The inversion is neatly suggested in the barn-scene, when Anna is wrapped in the silk-fringed paisley shawl belonging to Tom's mother.

Lawrence's creative authority, his novelistic skill, and his gift of comedy can be plentifully illustrated from the Tom and Anna sections. Early on, there is the resentfulness of the child 'with a face like a bud of apple-blossom, and glistening fair hair like thistle-down sticking out in straight, wild, flamy pieces, and very dark eyes' (p. 27). Then follows the uneasy, touching comedy of adjustment between stepfather and child, with exchanges rendered in dialogue superlatively simple and natural:

'Now then, Topsy, pop into thy bonnet.'
The child drew herself up, resenting the indignity of the address.
'I can't fasten my bonnet myself', she said haughtily.
'Not man enough yet,' he said, tying the ribbons under her chin with clumsy fingers. . . .
'You talk-nonsents', she said, re-echoing one of his phrases.
'*That* face shouts for th' pump', he said, and taking out a big red handkerchief, that smelled of strong tobacco, began wiping round her mouth.
'Is Kitty waiting for me?', she asked.
'Ay', he said. 'Let's finish wiping your face—it'll pass wi' a cat-lick.'
(p. 66)

The fresh humour and relish of this offsets the other tones in the exchanges, showing how well the novelist avoids over-insistence, avoids the schematic or the emotionally oppressive.

When the other tones in their relation are heard, Tom and Anna are boy-girl lovers, or unperplexed adults, innocents in the world of experience. It is the next step that alerts Lydia, when Tom seeks out the doctor's widow, Mrs. Forbes, his brother Alfred's mistress. Educated, with refined, artistic tastes, she moves for Tom in 'a polite visionary world'. He longs to make Anna into just such a lady: the sexual element in the relation is reaching a sharper definition. In a powerful, climactic scene, Lydia challenges Tom about his new desires, astonishing him by her insights (pp. 87–90). She voices his sense of having missed what he originally sought. The association of Alfred and Mrs. Forbes recalls his Matlock experience. Yet Lydia's action makes Tom realise how much he has fallen into expecting life simply to furnish forth its riches. She calls him to respond in love, not to submit; in their contact, she makes him 'passionately lovely to himself'. Tom recaptures self-esteem, living from his own centre, his relation with Lydia being completely renewed. So Anna is freed from exigent demands, and has her spontaneity released:

> Anna's soul was put at peace between them. She looked from one to the other, and saw them established to her safety, and she was free. She played between the pillar of fire and the pillar of cloud in confidence. . . . She was no longer called upon to uphold with her childish might the broken end of the arch. Her father and her mother now met to the span of the heavens, and she, the child, was free to play in the space beneath, between. (p. 92)

Tom finds the world remade, resurrected, in the passion of his marriage to Lydia. Travelling, searching, moving to the beyond is all in achieving relation. The perfected arc in the sky is seen only from the completed arch of an established, living bond. In despair at their disjunction, Tom had felt annulled by Lydia:

> He sat with every nerve, every vein, every fibre of muscle in his body stretched on a tension. He felt like a broken arch thrust sickeningly out from support. (p. 60)

This initially descriptive analogy, like so many parallel figures in the book, takes on impressive symbolic reference as it is shaped in a wide range of contexts. The sexual connotations of this complex of metaphors are annotated in the *Study of Thomas Hardy*. The column is said to represent man, and male aspiration; the arch or ellipse represents 'the female completeness containing this aspiration'. The arch is a reflection of the arc in the sky, signifying the journey to fulfilment which is 'to create a new knowledge of Eternity in the flux of Time'. In Blakean fashion, Lawrence finds immortality in the vividness of life, not in its loss. So Lydia addresses the drowned Tom Brangwen: 'I shared life with you, I belong in my own way to eternity'.

As Tom reviews this life in his reflections before Anna's wedding, he mixes pride, regret, puzzlement:

> What was missing in his life that, in his ravening soul, he was not satisfied? . . . What had he known but the long marital embrace with his wife! Curious that this was what his life amounted to. At any rate, it was something, it was eternal. (p. 124)

Though drawn always towards the home, Lydia within it, Tom feels little of a master, father, or husband, conscious of an 'ever-raging, ever-unsatisfied desire'. This unsettledness and precariousness, with its bitter, ironic undertones, is not index of failure in Tom and Lydia's marriage. It represents its openness, its capacity for growth, its ability to nourish in Anna the seeds of living in the next generation. Tom's anguish and pride, his unsatisfaction and self-awareness, give him a stature to match Lydia's fierce self-possession and mysterious serenity. (His complexity and his kind of heroism can be favourably brought out by comparison with Hardy's Gabriel Oak, or even George Eliot's Adam Bede.) In their balance of feeling, Lydia and Tom remain open to what is unknown, to what they may not comprehend:

> It was the entry into another circle of existence, it was the baptism to another life. . . . Everything was lost, and everything was found. The new world was discovered, it remained only to be explored. (p. 91)

The marriage, like the individual characters, is not subjected to a profit-loss accounting. The rhetoric that suggests what splendour they achieve is a non-ethical language, an idiom derived from that of the Bible, using as the major trope a journeying through the entrance to 'the infinite world, eternal, unchanging', transposing the quotidian into the mythical realm:

> They had passed through the doorway into the further space, where movement was so big, that it contained bonds and constraints and

labours, and still was complete liberty. She was the doorway to him, he to her. At last they had thrown open the doors, each to the other, and had stood in the doorways facing each other, whilst the light flooded out from behind on to each of their faces, it was the transfiguration, glorification, the admission. (p. 91)

2   Will and Anna

Anna Lensky's growing-up, her courtship and marriage to Will Brangwen give vivid dramatic impetus to the narrative's spiral. Polish by birth and name, she is reared in a Brangwen household. The impressive scene in the barn—distantly related to that in Hardy's *Far From The Madding Crowd*, chapter XXII—witnesses her assimilation of the traditional rhythms of living (pp. 73–76). Anna's alert intelligence marks her as a creature of consciousness, who resists the close, wordless home-atmosphere. Yet her encounter with Tom's nephew turns on her fascination with the dark Brangwen temperament: the intense, strange young man seems 'hovering on the edge of consciousness, ready to come in'. In a low key, this Sunday-morning sequence with the visit to church (pp. 102–109) sounds the notes of the Cathedral section. The pulsations and tense rhythms of their courtship and marriage are set in motion through the deftly comic inflections of the play of boy and girl attraction.

In the unpublished Foreword to *Women In Love*, Lawrence might well be describing the imaginative ethology of so many figures in *The Rainbow*:

Man struggles with his unborn needs and fulfilment. New unfoldings struggle up in torment in him, as buds struggle forth in the midst of a plant. Any man of real individuality tries to know and to understand what is happening, even in himself, as he goes along. This struggle for verbal consciousness should not be left out in art. It is a very great part of life. It is not superimposition of a theory. It is the passionate struggle into conscious being. (*PX II*, p. 276)

Tom Brangwen, tormented, unformed, had struggled to extend himself, to attain a fuller being. Will follows, a different enough nature, to reach new, sustaining forms. What the early Brangwens found in the unison of man, work, and nature, Will finds in craftwork, study, creative art. He seems to wed the vigour and vitality of the men to the knowledge and tastes of their women. He is stimulated, sometimes goaded, by the critical sharpness of Anna, the being of light to whom he is drawn. The illumination she brings him is signalled by a vision whose terms first recall the transformation of Tom and Lydia, and, more piquantly, anticipate those of Ursula's closing vision:

> He surveyed the rind of the world: houses, factories, trams, the discarded rind; people scurrying about, work going on, all on the discarded surface. An earthquake had burst it all from inside. It was as if the surface of the world had been broken away entire: Ilkeston, streets, church, people, work, rule-of-the-day, all intact; and yet peeled away into unreality; one's own being . . . suddenly became present, revealed, the permanent bedrock, knitted one rock with the woman one loved. (p. 146)

Selfhood is attained in the fulfilment of a passional relation. In the world of *The Rainbow*, everything is related, everything is distinct. Lawrence does not envision the universe, as perhaps Joyce does, as one vast particular. To create the vital flow and recoil of living and growing, there must be two poles, two forces of being in balance. This duality is the tension of every relation, as of every single psychic being. So Anna, fair, bright, quick, matches Will, dark, vital, intense; the mode of Love and that of Law seem to bring them to harmony. Watching their embrace, Tom is overwhelmed by the sense of time's curtailments. From the darkness of a rainy night, he sees them standing high in the lighted barn. The moment recalls that of his looking into the vicarage window, at the child Anna with her mother. More poignantly, it recalls the night he carried her out there to console her, while he fed the beasts:

> Outside, the rain slanted by in fine, steely, mysterious haste, emerging out of the gulf of darkness. (Will) held her in his arms, and he and she together seemed to be swinging in big, swooping oscillations, the two of them clasped together up in the darkness. (p. 114)

The symbolism of light and dark, sharply focused in this scene, is related and supported throughout the action by metaphors of the four elements, air, earth, fire and water. Almost any crystallisation of the meaning will involve such imagery of the elements, with a consistency rarely found in prose fiction. The evocation of the traditional mode of living—'So the Brangwens came and went'—the barn-scene, and Tom's visit to the vicarage, are outstanding instances. The sense in which these sequences can be called 'ritualistic' is suggested by Lawrence's discussion of what it is that gives life to a novel: 'In every great novel, who is the hero all the time? Not any of the characters, but some unnamed and nameless flame behind them all. . . . The felt but unknown flame stands behind all the characters, and in their words and gestures there is a flicker of the presence' (*The Novel/PX II*, pp. 416–426). The symbolism of Lawrence's novel works to create a sense of this divine, cosmic livingness, in and around the particularity of person, place, and event. The scenes are ritualistic when this macro-drama is enacted in the micro-drama of specific characters' words, gestures, and acts.

In the representation of the life of blood-intimacy, the major symbolism is that of the soil and the seasons, the earth itself. In Tom's visit to seek Lydia, on the night of the great wind, it is the symbolism of air that incarnates the cosmic livingness. In Tom's death by flood, the great flood of Creation is made a literal presence, its 'lovely and terrible waves' closing the Brangwen era. The harvest-field climax of Will and Anna's courtship brings into relation these varied, fundamental symbols. Metaphors of the four elements fashion the scene; the setting of harvest and night-time subtly suggests its affiliations with the life-mode it replaces. The large golden moon is itself a presence, a persona, a Being; it gives the action a suspension, a removed, essential atmosphere. Not that the scene is unanchored, indeterminate: it has time, place, detail, and could not occur at just any point in the relationship. Accidents of personality do begin to fall away, as in Tom and Lydia's courtship (closing the first chapter); but individuality and uniqueness are not being obliterated. As the moon irradiates all with a sense of mystery and otherness, the figures move into a realm of essential being, attaining mythic stature. Inner and outer are now made one, and the behaviour expresses a total meaning. The poetic suggestiveness of word and detail subtly links the personal and the mythic realms. Will's carving of Eve and angels, expressive of his response to Anna, provides the images describing the lovers' walk to the Marsh (p. 116). Will's role becomes mythic, that of unfallen Adam, a Son of God; Anna's is Eve, representing the Daughters of Men. The Biblical legend (*Genesis, 6*) becomes a major trope in the narrative—central and explicit in Ursula's story—crystallising the sacramental sense of the bond of passion between man and woman.

The sheaves scene is a very fine example of the subtle symbolic mode of this novel. Laurence Lerner calls it the most splendid scene in Lawrence's work, acclaiming it as 'the greatest love-scene in English fiction' (*The Truthtellers*, p. 204). He stresses the way the symbolism contains duality, the yielding and the holding apart of love. The scene is distinctive for other kinds of reconciliation, its harmonies of surface and depth, of objective and subjective. In the reaped field, the young lovers delight in their play of forming corn-stooks, turning it to love-play, sexual pursuit and capture. The human sexual impulses are in consonance with the natural, organic rhythms, to which indeed they give the crowning human form and significance:

> Into the rhythm of his work there came a pulse and a steadied purpose. He stooped, he lifted the weight, he heaved it towards her, setting it as in her, under the moonlit space . . . ever he drove her more nearly to the meeting. . . . There was only the moving to and fro in the moonlight, engrossed, the swinging in the silence, that was marked only by the splash of sheaves, and silence, and a splash of sheaves. And ever the splash of his sheaves broke swifter, beating up to hers. . . . (p. 119)

The density, the rhythmic development, and the compression of this section are remarkable; its poetic integrity is damaged by the omissions made. This close-woven texture of the language is evident in so many of the ritualistic climaxes of the action. The poised phrasing, the repetition, the parallelism, the appositive and the contrasting word groups all contribute to the finely imaginative rhythms. They enact, not describe, the meaning, creating an equivalence for the motions of nature and of human sexuality, incarnating the links of individual and cosmic rhythms. The central, controlling paradigm, more exactly than that of love-pursuit or courtship, is that of sexual consummation.

In a discarded section of an early version of *Women In Love* (PX II, pp. 92–108), Lawrence writes of two characters who are, to all intents and purposes, distant and detached: 'It was in the other world of the subconsciousness that the interplay took place, the interchange of spiritual and physical richness, the relieving of physical and spiritual poverty, without any intrinsic change of state in either'. In creating a form of notation for this complex interchange between characters like Will and Anna, the novelist hits against the paucity of ways to represent the carbon of the dynamic subconscious. The negative cast of the terms is sadly betraying—all prefixed by in-, un-, pre-, and sub-. To Lawrence, it all reflected an acceptance of primal creative vitality as it exists in a state of repression. As Ortega y Gasset affirms, the novelist must take account of the science of psychology, whatever its inadequacies. Lawrence felt only antipathy for Freudian concepts and psychoanalysis, fashioned as they were by repressive forms of modern civilization. It was blasphemy to represent the form of man's unconscious as 'a cave of unspeakable horrors', a cellarage of repressions. The 'active human first-mind'— Lawrence desperately sought periphrases to help the rescue—is a fountain-head of creativity, desire, and spontaneity. No negative idioms can conceal its native divinity.

The argument with Garnett, with its carbon-coal-diamond analogies, controverts the concept of the 'old stable ego', in literature and in life. This monadic concept, with its concomitants of personality and the will, seems to overvalue mental, ideal consciousness. In novels, it dictates plot-patterning based on the play in relationships of moral principles and ideals. Crises of conscience and resolutions by moral choice became 'the usual resting places, eminences, and consummations of the usual novel'. (Virginia Woolf uses these terms, remarking their notable absence from Lawrence's novels.) Lawrence saw the paramountcy of the personality, the will, and the mental consciousness as an expression of the purposes of society. Fiction was a social art-form in far too constricted a sense. In characterisation, for example, Lawrence saw that some kinds of concern with individuality and the idiosyncratic were antipathetic to concern for radical human differences and uniqueness. In the name of human spontaneity, he deplores 'the old-fashioned human element—which causes one to conceive a character in a certain moral scheme and make him consistent' (*L.I*, p. 281). He violently rejects the Bennett–Wells–Galsworthy formal traditionalism, 'their pernicious, ossiferous, skin-and-grief form'. Such narratives deployed 'awfully lifelike and lifeless figures' in endless treatment of manners, morals, money, and class. Galsworthy's characters are alive as social beings only:

> Whence arises this repulsion from the Forsytes, this emotional refusal to have them identified with our common humanity? . . . . It is because they seem to us to have lost caste as human beings and to have sunk to the level of social being. . . . He may give away all he has to the poor and still reveal himself as a social being swayed finally and help-lessly by the money-sway, and by the social moral, which is inhuman. (*PX I*, pp. 540–541)

Lawrence traces the interest in personality, in the individualising traits of appearance and temperament, to the concern with status and material things, with the social moral. His diagnosis is of a fissure of being in man, a rending of the subjective and the objective consciousness. (He indicates how the lyrical novelist, preoccupied with an internal world, is acceding to such a dichotomy as much as the descriptive, realistic writer.) Lawrence's positive response, as theorist and novelist, is to shape a psychology and a mode of characterisation that attempts a unison of subjective and objective consciousness. Such a unified or organic individuality is what he seeks to indicate in explications of the 'dynamic first-mind' and man's 'vital sanity'. This is the realm of carbon which the novelist seeks to represent: what people are 'inhumanly, physiologically, materially'. The hyperbole springs from impatience with the tendency to equate a man with the distinguishing marks of his social being. The 'Futuristic' terminology is a gesture towards a psychology of man's unique wholeness, what Lawrence calls being 'man-alive'.

Even the greater artist may confuse personality and social character with radical individuality, according to Lawrence, when he refers specifically to Thomas Hardy:

> This setting behind the small action of his protagonists the terrific action of unfathomed nature ... is the quality Hardy shares with the great writers, Shakespeare or Sophocles or Tolstoi; setting a smaller system of morality, the one grasped and formulated by the human consciousness, within the vast, uncomprehended and incomprehensible morality of nature or of life itself, surpassing human consciousness. The difference is ... in Hardy or Tolstoi the lesser human morality, the mechanical system is actively transgressed, and holds, and punishes the protagonist, whilst the greater morality is only passively, negatively transgressed. (*PX I*, pp. 419–420)

The social ethic is a lesser morality insofar as its values are a shield against nature's unfathomed moral forces. The finest moral values of a community may be largely accessible through its manners. Yet the 'greater unwritten morality' may call for an Anna Karenina to be patient, to wait until 'by virtue of a greater right, she could take what she needed from society'. Only detachment from system can sustain Vronsky's individuality, while he and Anna create 'a new colony of morality'.

Lawrence's score for the sentiments of the stable ego—especially the doggy amorousness and the 'Pa-assion' of the Forsytes and their like—is not part of any championship of a Dionysian release of feelings. He protested to Garnett (*L.I*, p. 263): 'I don't care much more about accumulating objects in the powerful light of emotion, and making a scene of

them. I have to write differently.' An acute comment by Virginia
Woolf on a scene of Lawrence's singles out this difference:

> Their bodies become incandescent, glowing, significant, as in other
> books a passage of emotion burns in that way. For the writer it seems
> the scene is possessed of a transcendental significance. (*The Moment*)

Virginia Woolf might have been describing the sheaves scene, or many
parallel passages in the novel. That the characters alluded to are in *Sons
and Lovers* suggests Lawrence was already moving on from the firm,
vivid style of the early work. Woolf's comment, 'as in other books a
passage of emotion burns in that way', crystallises the point that the
intensity is parallel to, but not identifiable with, that of emotion. It is
the distinctive symbolic mode which controls response, precluding the
translation of the intensities as ultimates of emotion. They open up vistas
of significance beyond that of the play of human feelings. Alan Friedman
suggests this in comparing the sheaves scene with Hardy's sheaves-
binding scene in *Tess of the D'Urbervilles* (ch. XIV). Outward description
is there made to evoke interior meanings; Hardy's dramatic mode
reaches beneath the events for a symbolic truth.

The quick of self, the intuitive underconscious: this is co-existent, co-
vital with the individual organism. It is not a store of potential or of
unformed, weltering emotions. This primal core has its own centre of
responsibility, its own totality of awareness. The stream of consciousness
for Lawrence is not an aspect, not a partial or an emergent current of
semi-articulation. It is itself a complete form of livingness:

> Consciousness, however, does not take rise in the nerves and the brain.
> . . . Every speck of protoplasm, every living cell is *conscious*. . . . And all
> the time they give off a stream of consciousness which flows along the
> nerves and keeps us spontaneously alive. (*PX I*, p. 767)

This redefined stream of consciousness, an organic totality of being, is
to be dramatised by the novelist. The section *Anna Victrix* shows how
this is achieved in the depiction of the married life of Anna and Will.
Day-to-day living is crisply, fully realised, and the naturalistic density
shows no retreat is involved in registering the total consciousness of the
partners. There is no withdrawal into a fugitive or subjective realm. Yet
the pressures of the intuitive, vital selfhood impinge electrically, as in the
incidents of the housework, the tea-party, the path-making. The lightest
gesture or simplest word, far from being superficial sketching in of

temperament, can manifest the interplay of deep psychic needs, the interchange of bodily and spiritual poverty or richness.

These extended, apparently naturalistic sequences take on the kind of reverberation felt elsewhere through the imagery and symbolism by virtue of what Alan Friedman calls the 'subjective correlative'. The phrase 'objective correlative' was T. S. Eliot's, to define the means of expressing emotion in the form of art: it indicates 'a set of objects, a situation, a chain of events which shall be the formula of that *particular* emotion'. The external facts, terminating in sensory experience, are paramount in the novel-genre, its life-blood, in a way not true for drama or poetry. Lawrence's remarks on making a scene by accumulating objects in the light of a powerful emotion offer some parallel to Eliot's definition. It represents a mode of fiction which he associates with the primacy of individual feeling, and with inevitable emphasis on a moral schema. Attempting to dislodge these priorities, the strategy of *The Rainbow* is to displace one side of the objects–emotion correlation. The narrative maintains the genre's focus on sensory experience, and its respect for external facts. But it also provokes an imbalance: the 'responses' of the characters do not neatly match a confronted act or situation. The responses are not simply externally referential, since they themselves are now made into objects, situations, events. In Alan Friedman's phrase, they are the 'subjective correlative'. They become internally referential, in that they become analogies for the preverbal dynamic first mind.

The strategy of the 'subjective correlative' is prompted by the †† novelist's all-but-impossible task: to reveal primal being in and behind ordinary exchanges, the daily collisions of temperaments. The complexity and density of the action is the outcome of this relation of carbon to coal or diamond, of essential to accidental, of esoteric to exoteric. The honeymoon sequence amply witnesses the triumphs of the novelist's answer to the formidable task. A scene will move along, presenting what seems like the easily predictable turns of a relationship, its nervous arguments and mutual adjustments:

'You need some work to *do*', she said. 'You ought to be at work. Can't you do something?'
His soul only grew the blacker. His condition now became complete, the darkness of his soul was thorough. Everything had gone: he remained complete in his own tense, black will. He was now unaware of her. She did not exist. His dark, passionate soul had recoiled upon

itself, and now, clinched and coiled round a centre of hatred, existed in its own power . . . She shuddered from him . . . His will seemed grappled upon her. (pp. 148–149)

If this were the language of feeling, of the play of emotions, then it would be open to such objections as J. I. M. Stewart's, that the flux of passion is rendered by 'a constant extremity of statement which becomes wearing'. The extreme quality is clearly deliberate; the bold simplicity of such metaphors as now occur contributes further to this functional hyperbole. As Friedman suggests, the ultimacy is of something beyond feeling. The apparent 'emotions' of the passage are themselves correlatives for something else, something further.

A term from rhetoric, 'auxesis', can suggest here the consistent stylistic heightening of language, the distension of word and phrase to release the new perceptions of meaning. This auxetic idiom is to suggest the nature and power of the psychic life: 'But our thoughts have generally such an obscure implicit language, that it is the hardest thing in the world to make them speak out distinctly' (*Exercises*, 3rd Earl of Shaftesbury, early eighteenth century). The novelist must make them speak out distinctly, translating 'thoughts' here as the gestures and intentions of the essential self. So of Will Brangwen, in his thorough darkness of soul, there seems to be withdrawal: 'He was now unaware of her. She did not exist.' Yet he also hangs on to her, threatens her obscurely: 'His will seemed grappled upon her.' This would be contradiction only in the realm of daylight feelings. The paradoxes are the tensional motions in 'the passional secret places of life'. So there is no wrench, no disjunction, when Anna's conciliatory 'Haven't you made it nice?' is followed by:

He looked up at her, with that fixed expressionless face and unseeing eyes which shocked her, made her go dazed and blind. Then he turned away. She saw his slender, stooping figure groping. A revulsion came over her. She went indoors. (p. 149)

The situation is antipodal to that of the sheaves scene, and is antipodal in style of language and narrative presentation. There is no direct rendering of all-out emotional states, no delineation of the exaggerations of characters' feelings. Certainly, there has to be admitted an element of mannerism, a degree of jargon: characters go dazed, blind, or dead, are tortured, lacerated, perfected. This is the overspill of a necessary insistence and absoluteness, a price paid in the compulsion of a new constructing of reality. For, like metaphors and poetic imagery in general, this idiosyncratic idiom prompts the reader to seek a sense in which it is valid. The auxesis transports the action and its meanings to a realm of the absolute, far beyond the limits of normal reference. The insistence and the hyperbole create a sense of ultimacy, a boundary-world, in which the norms of customary feeling and behaviour have no validity.

This is part of the analytical, 'far less visualised' style, the 'exhaustive method', which Lawrence struggled with like a foreign language (*L.I*, p. 203). Perhaps, in English fiction, only *Wuthering Heights* provides some parallel, in exchanges between Catherine and Heathcliff, to the tone and effect of these scenes in *The Rainbow*. With Emily Brontë and Lawrence, as with European and Russian novelists, implications concerning moral imagination and sensibility are contained, and sometimes engulfed, in the registration of deeply-rooted impulse and profound inner tensions. Such a fugitive, central core of being defines human + nature for these artists.

The 'obscure implicit language' of the intuitive quick of self is + shadowed forth in the inflections of Anna and Will's commonplace exchanges. Daylight words have here tentacular roots reaching into the core of primal being. The emotions that attend these slight exchanges, by their very dissonance and disproportion to anything said or done, compel the realisation that they refer to some other source. They analogise what cannot be represented other than by further obliqueness, allusion, or figurative language. One special effect is the way an imperfect tense is suggested, giving an air of recurrence to a specific relation. The language loosens the sense of time, creating a flexibility, a ranging between times and places. A further fluidity is in the use of totemic or emblematic imagery, as in the allusions to snake, mole, toad, and hawk. This last, the hawk-figure (p. 159), becomes a metaphoric focus of perceptions about the whole relationship. It climaxes references to Will's eyes, head, and movements over a hundred pages or so. It moves the significations into a realm free of time, space, and habitual terms of cause and effect.

The hyperbolic idiom is an important characteristic of the language of *The Rainbow*, part of the 'analytical' and 'exhaustive' method deliberately fashioned by Lawrence. Perhaps some degree of disapproval comes from the reader's unwillingness to extend to prose fiction the intensive focus he may bring to poetry. Certainly the sheer bulk of a novel works against an attempt to give its texture the density of good verse. Other kinds of disapproval of the idiom as obsessive and over-wrought seem to go with dislike of the kind of insight that the idiom subserves and expresses. The reader who rejects the characters' intensity and high pitch of feeling can ultimately only be referred to the gauge of experience; and, initially, to the witness of other literature, novels, poems, plays. Arnold Kettle, remarking on the 'uncommon, disproportionate' intensity, nevertheless finds the novelist's 'curious, intense convention' a remarkable, impressive mode for rendering the interplay and conflict of personalities. He singles out its non-naturalistic detail, its repetition, rhythm, imagery, and its 'insistent symbolic-seeming words'. The long section he quotes (from ch. III) as the finest account of the marriage-relation found in the English novel includes all these features of the Laurentian language. Kettle concludes that such an idiom will more fully and deeply present relationship than what he calls 'the colder terms of a fully rationalized prose'.

The superlative skill of the book's symbolic mode, its high-water mark, is evident in the visit to Lincoln Cathedral. That it is climactic, deeply and totally revelatory of Will and Anna, helps to explain its chronological displacement—attributed to the first year of marriage, it is recounted much later. What precedes it, especially in *Anna Victrix*, is palpably felt in this confrontation; in turn, retroactively, the whole marriage-relation is re-assessed. There is a startling sense of disclosure, of complete revelation of being. The sequence gathers up not only the threads of their passional connection, but many major concerns of the extended action of the book. Narratively, dramatically and poetically, the Cathedral is the centre of the work. The explorations, the imaginative 'findings' of *The Rainbow* all lead in to and lead out of this symbolic, nodal complex.

The springboard is a visit to Baron Skrebensky and his second (Venetian-English) wife. Their world of the 'fine deliberate response', a free element in which each person can be detached, ironical, gracious, recalls the world Tom Brangwen glimpsed in his Matlock encounters. Anna's immediate response is a sharpened irony towards Will. Yet his uncritical absorption, his ecstasy—with its strong sexual element—are not just fodder for his wife's keen-edged rationality. His spirit indeed soars, attains a consummation:

> In a little ecstasy he found himself in the porch, on the brink of the unrevealed. He looked up to the lovely unfolding of the stone. He was to pass within to the perfect womb. . . . His soul leapt up into the gloom, into possession, it reeled, it swooned with a great escape, it

quivered in the womb, in the hush and gloom of fecundity, like seed of procreation in ecstasy.

. . . Away from time, always outside of time! . . . Containing birth and death, potential with all the noise and transition of life, the cathedral remained hushed, a great involved seed, whereof the flower would be radiant life inconceivable, but whose beginning and whose end were the circle of silence. (p. 198)

Will's response is implicitly validated by its notation in terms that repeat those of the honeymoon (ch. VI, p. 141, paras. 8–11). This identifying of terms does not merely suggest displacement of feeling in Will, or the force of sublimation. For Anna also is swept along: 'She too was overcome with wonder and awe. She followed him in his progress'. The directly sexual cast and tone of Will's experience is not at all reductive, not at all an ironic undercutting of his exaltation. Nor does it betray in the novelist an incapacity to register such intensity of feeling without resort to measuring all by the values of an obsessive concern. The novel itself, by this stage of the narrative, has fashioned images of completeness in which the sexual, the natural, and the religious are inextricable.

In the expository *Psychoanalysis and the Unconscious*, one of the ways man attains knowledge is described thus: 'From the sympathetic centre of the breast, as from a window, the unconscious goes forth, seeking its object, to dwell upon it. This . . . primal objective knowledge . . . we call the treasure of the heart' (p. 229). Will's perception is of this sort: 'His very breast seemed to open its doors to watch for the great church.' In worship as in physical passion, Will brings, not a special part, but his whole self. His intense consummation is dark, physical, and mystical. It disregards the force and richness of all the metaphors to suggest that 'the mentalised, idealising, unphysical quality of his "feelings" is brilliantly conveyed' (Coveney, p. 329). In the sensuous, lush phrases and the incantatory rhythms, Will's response is not just adumbrated, pointed to. It is bodily there: the experience itself is created, an experience of ecstatic union. As George Ford asserts, its reality is attested by the participation of the empathetic reader. The main analogy between religious and sexual union is a means, not an end: the passage symbolically enacts a religious experience of the wholeness of union. Father W. Tiverton compares the seed-root-flower symbolism of the oneness of time (pp. 198–199) with the rose symbolism of *Four Quartets*. He concludes: 'Here perhaps is Lawrence's most sympathetic statement, and rejection, of the classic, Catholic scheme.'

Anna's rationality and scepticism disenchant Will, who has now to see what the Church excludes. The rainbow of the Cathedral's 'jewelled gloom' (pp. 198–199) betokens a numinous oneness, obliterating diversity and multiplicity, eliminating all oppositions of blood and spirit. The Gothic arch, expressive of man's imperfection, betokens fulfilment in the soul's separation, its ecstatic unison with the godhead. Neither now, to Will, seems preferable to 'the whole blue rotunda of the day', or to a Greek temple, open to winds and sky. The rainbow outside the Cathedral links earth to sky, sky to earth again: its unity maintains motion and diversity. It signals change and becoming, human fulfilment in nature and in time.

These images and emblems are summations in metaphor of the arguments in which Will and Anna move ever further apart. Though Anna argues destructively, to beat down her husband, she also beats back an insistent tide of passion, her own instinct to participate and to respond as Will does. Her 'profane laughter' of 'malicious triumph', pleased at her 'own very littleness', partly betrays the impulse to freedom which authorised her antagonism to monistic absolutes. Reaction is shown to take her so far that she appears to reject not just Christian practice and belief, but the religious sense itself. Later she admits, though only to herself, that 'she had some new reverence for that which he wanted' (p. 202).

A central concern of the novel is this principle of balance, equipoise, polarity. Every principle throughout is seen in terms of dynamic balance. This is so in the psychology of the characters, the presentation of their sexuality, the depiction of society, and of man's relation to nature and to the cosmos. The total structure of the Cathedral sequence evinces this patterning and poise of forces. The spiritual force of Will's experience is disinterestedly created; its mysterious power, ecstasy, and exaltation are fully dramatised, experienced by the reader. There is no simple gesturing towards a partly comprehended experience. Will adventures in spirit and in consciousness, the eyes in his chest do see treasures; unlike Anna, Will can 'be cast at last . . . upon the shore of the unknown'. At first entry, 'foreigner' to Anna, as her mother was to Tom, Will is associated with images of vitality, swift intensity, and vivid darkness. His strengths, intuitions, potentialities are adumbrated; he seeks in Anna the alertness, the sharp awareness of the daylight world. There are strange twists and turns in the struggle to achieve balance in himself and in his marriage. His corrosive passion for Anna is partly a wish to possess her totally, partly a wish to surrender himself totally. Will seems to be one of 'the great mergers . . . who love to extremes' (S.C.A.L., p. 182), and thus ever finding passionate fulfilment beyond him, rages in unsatisfaction.

For a quintessential condition for balance in relationship is insisted upon in the term 'polarity'. There has to be distinctness of being before there can be union. Lawrence's despair and disdain—articulated in his Whitman essay (S.C.A.L.)—is not of merging as such, but of connection that unbalances, when the oppositions collapse, fuse into unison. In the consummation of the marriage, isolated in the cottage, Will wonders at Anna's recklessness, independence, superb indifference. The persistent imagery of new seed, of the kernel and rind, along with images of the flood and a new world (pp. 140–141) attend the birth of Will's sensual self. His dark, intense being, however, makes him absorbent, dependent, unable to set the new self in relation to the quotidian. The protracted duel, with its fluctuations of intense hatred and passion, reaches one climax in Anna's dance, alone, naked, pregnant (a scene 'to which exception was *particularly* taken' by the magistrate—L.I, p. 615). She dances to signify her apartness, her individual being: not to mock Will, nor to signal man's exclusion from childbirth and motherhood. She forces him in bitterness to learn to be alone, single, independent. He is born again, having besides 'a relative self' a sense of 'an absolute self' (p. 187).

As Anna rests content in the warm domesticity of mothering her five children, Will chafes in dissatisfaction, unable to blend the elements of his living. He questions his life, probes the content of his purposes, with family, with work, with religion. 'The altar was the mystic door . . . but now . . . it was too narrow, it was false.' Family, sexual passion, his work: they remain in disjunction. What real balance and impersonality is achieved in his relation with Anna comes about in a surprising way. The attempted seduction of a Nottingham girl, called Jennie, rouses and changes Will; Anna responds to the challenge of his strangeness:

> He lived in a passion of sensual discovery with her for some time—it was a duel: no love, no words, no kisses even, only the maddening perception of beauty consummate, absolute through touch. (p. 233)

Precluding tenderness, this sensual intoxication obliterates responsibility, being extreme and annulling personality. In an obscure way, it appeases Will's thirst for the extreme of the Absolute that he sought in the Cathedral. He feels now that the self is absolute, that he grasps the whole world. Physical sensation, heightened by a detachment of each from the self, becomes an Absolute Beauty they mutually explore. 'They were neither of them quite personal, quite defined as individuals.' (p. 353)

Falteringly, as a consequence of this third kind of rebirth, Will tries to give form to his living. He runs evening classes, eventually becoming a handicraft instructor; he even resumes his own carving and creative work. He still aspires to give some utterance to himself, to fashion a new balance. Yet it is still only a resolution of sorts: in himself, and in his marriage, the equipoise is of too few opposites, and excludes too much. The alertness and sceptical play of awareness that Anna brought has been blunted in the warm complacency of family and home, which now has some of the drowsiness of the life at Marsh Farm. The new immersion in intense physical passion renews Will and Anna's relation only in a limited way. Their marriage fails to link light and dark, Law and Love, and begins to lose impetus.

The concept of marriage is central in *The Rainbow*, as in *Women In Love*, since it acts as the type of all relationship. The essential seriousness the gravity even, of sexual passion in marriage is in its creating and expressing the whole range of man's possible relations, to others, to nature, to the universe. The marriages, though specific in dramatic form, are far removed from being particular studies or case-histories. What the couples achieve in passional marriage is not referable to matters of temperament or character. The context for each marriage is vitally important: a context created in the narrative strategies and in the rhetoric of metaphor, symbol, and myth. The dimensions are of too ample a scale to suggest even a subtle form of social determinism: it is never a matter of the actual possibilities of living suggested for the 1850's or the early 1900's. Into the nominal seventy-five years (*c.* 1830–1905) of the story, the novelist compresses a total time-scheme of human development. Hence the quintessentially poetic form of the book: it evokes man's movement through history. Alfred Brangwen's first generation is suggestive of patriarchal, tribal existence; Tom Brangwen's generation is one of exodus, movement from the land, renewal by exogamy. Will Brangwen's generation, losing the religious instinct of the forbears, establish the church, only to see it wither under their own rational intelligence. Each 'generation' comprehends massive time-sweeps, each ritualistic and symbolic scene evokes whole eras of history. Finally, Ursula Brangwen, singly, independently, lives through the agonies of the modern consciousness, compelled to create all values anew, from within.

The Biblical tropes of flood and rainbow mark off the end of each era; the wanderings of the Israelites, the Chosen People, provide the extended background image in each section. The figurative language of *Anna Victrix* after the dance is crowded with allusions to ark, rock, flood, and walking on the water (see especially pp. 183 ff.). As with their quarrels and sexual conflict, the symbolism focuses the perils that encircle Anna and Will. Living is problematic in ways unknown to the earlier genera-tions; their awareness of almost total loss, manifested in the Cathedral scenes, adds bravery and poignancy to what resolution to conflict they do attain. As Kinkead-Weekes concludes: 'We can now see more clearly that the new intensities of Anna and Will, while making the marriage of opposites more difficult to achieve, also show up the limitations of Tom and Lydia. Will's religious and aesthetic intensity, Anna's rational intelligence and self-awareness, represent a greater range of human possibility as well as difficulty.'

Anna, with the child Ursula, and with Will close by, is at least graced by a sight of what is to come. She never accomplished the bird-soul flight to high freedom, settling instead 'in her builded house, a rich woman'. The doorway to fulfilment that she saw in Will remains half-open only: she feels herself to be 'a door and a threshold', through whom 'another soul was coming'. If she and Will have not fared forward to the promised land, they have at least the grace and blessing of looking to its advent. God's beauty and glory, and the sign of the Covenant, were witnessed by the rainbow after the flood. Moses after the wanderings for so many years was granted from Pisgah a view of his people's fulfilment. An overlap of these allusions enriches the symbolism of the archway:

> She was straining her eyes to something beyond. And from her Pisgah mount, which she had attained, what could she see? A faint, gleaming horizon, a long way off, and a rainbow like an archway, a shadow-door with faintly coloured coping above it. . . .
> . . . Dawn and sunset were the feet of the rainbow that spanned the day, and she saw the hope, the promise. (p. 192)

So also the significance of Anna's dancing is intensified by inter-linking of allusion, symbol, and metaphor. She certainly celebrates her independent being; yet that includes celebration of the child-to-be, named after the saint Ursula. The dancing is fine, strange, exultant, dedicated to the Lord—Anna remembers how David danced before the Lord. Beyond this, however, as George Ford indicates, she dances because she is mother of a prophet: 'Evidently (Anna) is cast as a fore-runner, a Moses, a John, or even a Mary. The scene . . . is actually a modern Magnificat'. When Anna first knows she is pregnant, the latter analogy is directly invoked—though its selfconsciousness works against its impact there (p. 175—but cf. 'the Angel of the Presence', p. 167). The men outside the cottage on the wedding-night, led by Tom, sing a Nativity hymn.

The final analogy to clinch the sense that Will and Anna's child will be heroic, a leader and a prophet, is one that is curiously anticipated in *Sons and Lovers*. Mrs. Morel ponders the future of her child, watching the hills blaze in the red sunset. She imagines the shocks of corn bowing to him, fancying he may become a Joseph. 'She thrust the infant forward to the crimson, throbbing sun' (p. 37). At this moment she names him Paul; his family nickname makes it obvious that she thinks of the apostle. In *The Rainbow*, Anna faces 'the blazing close' of a fiery winter sun, and the metaphoric allusions identify the child she holds up to it as God's witness, like Meshach, Shadrach, and Abednego, unharmed by the fire of the furnace into which they were cast for rejecting false images of God (*Daniel*, 3):

> The child she might hold up, she might toss the child into the furnace, the child might walk there, amid the burning coals and the incandescent roar of heat, as the three witnesses walked with the angel in the fire. (p. 193)

3 Ursula

Throughout *The Rainbow*, as an instance of its principle of continuity-in-discontinuity, there occurs an action of paramount importance in Laurentian thinking, the parental pressure on the child. This pressure readily serves to show the radically dual nature of act and situation. Tom Brangwen as a child is roused, awakened from lapsing into the life of blood-intimacy, by the urgent, questing spirit of his mother. His confusion, awkwardness, his sense of being guilty of his own nature, all follow from this. Yet so do his perceptions of what makes living fine and vivid, of what a free existence may be. In turn, Anna's relations to her stepfather Tom reflect the varying forms of this pressure. The girl evades some of her mother's heavy insistence by turning to him; yet, in part, he seeks from Anna an unquestioning, quasi-maternal affection. In her married relations with Will Brangwen, Anna seeks beyond the Brangwen dark potency, the participation in the affairs of the outer world—for which her father Paul Lensky had paid by slighting wife and child. Perhaps, too, Anna's early arousal by these parental pressures, the implicit demands for mutuality, stimulate her pert, childish 'fawceness', and her later strong-mindedness, her rationality and scepticism.

Ursula's childhood and adolescence naturally reveal similar lines of force, with more complicated outcome. Tom's childhood stresses were contained within the larger stability of the way of life at Marsh Farm. His marriage to Lydia achieved a resolution which gave Anna a greater freedom, though a vestigial, obscure jealousy dies down only upon her marriage. The irresolutions, the dissatisfactions of Will and Anna's marriage set up more complicated strains and demands for their first child. The representation of these is more comprehensive, more complicated, more intense, and subsumes the earlier sequences. The dramatic incisiveness of Will Brangwen's relationship with his daughter Ursula is the most telling, internal test of what is offered elsewhere as the resolution of his marriage to Anna. As much as anything else, the Will–Ursula connection is shaped by his incompletion and unfulfilment. The narrative, with some hesitancy and indetermination, suggests that the extreme sensuality of the latter phase of the marriage creates a new sense of purpose in the husband. He returns to the daylight world of men, work, cities, becoming craftsman, artist, and educator. The causal connection is asserted, but hardly fashioned in narrative, dramatic form. Its tentativeness is clearly revealed by the authentic notation of a father–child connection which suggests that the emergence of the socially-purposive Will masks frustrations and inadequacies.

From the first, Will has barely acknowledgeable emotion about the child: 'It was so strong, and came out of the dark of him.' His claim on the child at the moment of birth (p. 189) is rationalised as compensation for Anna's clear disappointment—which proves transient. For the baby is the extruded vulnerable innocent self of Will, that he promptly seeks to re-possess. Much more agonisingly than Tom did, he needs reassurance: Ursula gives him such self-verification. While he feels 'right' in his dark sensuous underworld, 'in the outside, upper world, he was wrong'.

In Will, Anton Skrebensky, and Tom Brangwen II, the artist is exploring strata of motive and behaviour that will finally produce the powerfully condensed representation of Gerald Crich.

The child Ursula's modes of apprehension become father-centred; Anna was older, more capable of resistance, in the earlier, parallel situation. *Fantasia of the Unconscious* (ch. X) comments on such a situation, when the dormant higher centres of sympathy and cognition are artificially stimulated into response 'by the adult personal love-emotion and love-will . . . in a quite young child, sometimes even in an infant. This is a holy obscenity.' Home and parental pressure are the most mischievous: 'There is the most intimate mesh of love, love-bullying, and "understanding" in which a child is entangled' (pp. 116–117). This is exactly the situation, superbly and specifically rendered, of Will and Ursula. He bases his life on the child, 'on her support and her accord'. This 'dynamic spiritual incest' (*Fant.* p. 118) creates a considerable imbalance throughout Ursula's development. Yet the incisive reprobatory tone of the *Fantasia* discussion must be set against the subtly ambivalent dramatisation of situation and consequences in the action of the novel. With a remarkably responsible sense of what injures the soul's health, Lawrence the artist does not accede to a moralistic over-readiness to see human imbalance only in terms of loss. Ursula's career, more lucidly and more eloquently than Will Brangwen's, explores the ways in which imbalance, excess, or viciousness can be incorporated in the quest for fulfilment.

The supercharged feelings between adult and child are disclosed by the novel's pointed use of seemingly minor incident—Ursula's upsetting hymn-books, or trampling the flower-beds. All the excessive expectations of the adult play through the scene of setting potatoes (pp. 219–220). (This is an ironic-pathetic reduction of the Brangwen work-rhythms, so potently realised at the book's opening.) The tender intimacy has been soured, blighted, as the father frantically hits out in blind disillusion, the child numbed and overwhelmed at incomprehensible demands. She retreats, all she can do, to live in 'the little separate world of her own violent will':

She asserted herself only. There was now nothing in the world but her own self. . . . She came to believe in the outward malevolence that was against her . . . . that even her adored father was part of this malevolence. And very early she learned to harden her soul in resistance and denial of all that was outside her, harden herself upon her own being. (p. 221)

Ursula absorbs into her being the destructive shocks from this over-close affiliation, this precocious arousal. Again, the ordinary incident is sketched, a commonplace situation, beneath which are felt 'the vibrations of a deep and complex human disaster' (William Walsh's phrase, in his very fine study of this section). These vibrations are seismically registered in the incident of Will's leaping to swim from a canal-bridge, with the naked child on his shoulders; and in the incident of the fairground swing-boats, which Will sends to a terrifying height, making Ursula violently sick. This is the outcome of their continuous 'curious taunting intimacy', and of Will's sadistic, destructive, deathly instincts.

Cold, isolating disillusion comes upon Ursula for the first time; she turns away, her soul deadened, and moves towards Anna. After a time, Will effects an unthinking transfer to the girl Jennie he pursues in Nottingham: 'Her childishness whetted him keenly.' Her vulnerability sharply appeals to his unresolved feelings about Ursula. What might seem, in brief summary, a vicious and sordid sequence, leads in fact to a renewal of connections between Will and Anna. The premeditated sensuality with Jennie is a bolder release of feelings about Ursula than the displacement towards Mrs. Forbes of Tom Brangwen's less intense feelings about the young Anna. As Colin Clarke insists, dismissive moral judgement is not invited, and the human value of Will's attitudes and experience not easily established: 'The perversity and destructiveness are fully conceded, and artistically, fully realised; but so is the beauty, the "amazing beauty and pleasure". As so often in Lawrence's work, the effect is one of double exposure: we register the impulse to destruction even while we acknowledge the enhancement of life.' The Jennie sequence which prompts this 'amazing beauty and pleasure' of Will's and Anna's new phase is patently a displacement of feelings about Ursula. Insofar as the aroused, purposive Will is reborn of this dark baptism of extreme sensation and lust, the Jennie–Ursula collocation does lead to the suggestive close: 'Only he was fondest of Ursula. Somehow, she seemed to be at the back of his new night-school venture.' The mysterious confluence of the tributaries is marked at the resolution of the chapter, as the narrative swings away from Will and Anna, and with Tom's death, centres on the new world and on Ursula:

> She seemed to run in the shadow of some dark, potent secret of which she would not, of whose existence even she dared not become conscious, it cast such a spell over her, and so darkened her mind. (p. 236)

The play of interconnection between eras is lived out in the mutual responses of the generations. Ursula's relations with her grandparents, Lydia and Tom Brangwen, show some of the living human forms through which the desires of the spirit are acted out. The narrative does not hypostatise a Life Spirit or Cosmic Force which shapes larger purposes through the agency of individuals. In a sense, each generation gives its successors the means to set it at a discount, to assess and use it, to dismiss it. So, at seventeen years old, Ursula turns on her favourite *Book of Genesis* with Anna-like mockery:

> Multiplying and replenishing the earth bored her. Altogether it seemed merely a vulgar and stock-raising sort of business. 'And you (Noah and his sons) be ye fruitful and multiply; bring forth abundantly in the earth, aud multiply therein.' In her soul she mocked at this multiplication, every cow becoming two cows, every turnip ten turnips. (p. 323)

The patriarchal, tribal Brangwen life, passed on from Adam–Alfred to Noah–Tom, provides comic metaphors for a schoolgirl's witty scorn. The profoundly earnest, mythical symbols of the earlier generations do not command her sensibility. Anna's mocking reflections anticipate her response to encounters with Anthony Schofield (pp. 415–417). Vital, graceful, yet animal-like, absorbed in the life that surrounds him, he recalls all the best of Tom Brangwen's way of living. She longs for Schofield 'to become real to her':

> All her life, at intervals, she returned to the thought of him and of that which he offered. But she was a traveller on the face of the earth, and he was an isolated creature living in the fulfilment of his own senses. (p. 417)

Ursula's relation with Schofield makes her discriminations and ironic assessments into vital, specific choices, into experiences that are lived through.

To ignore history, as Lawrence said, and as he shows in so many ways, is to omit one's fulfilment in the past. Ursula's relations with her grandparents and with Anthony Schofield show that she makes no such error. Through Lydia, she is in touch with other versions and forms of the past. Tom's widow seems unchanged after a quarter-century:

> She seemed always to haunt the Marsh rather than to live there . . . she remained a stranger within the gates, in some ways fixed and impervious, in some ways curiously refining. She caused the separateness

and individuality of all the Marsh inmates, the friability of the household. (p. 239)

In this last respect, Lydia's sensibility and influence are directly anti-
thetical to those of Tom and Anthony Schofield. Lydia's attitude to her
growing sons, forcing them into independence, rejecting their emotional
pressures, is the inverse of Will's treatment of Ursula—and implicitly a
critical-imaginative comment on Gertrude Morel's attitudes in *Sons and
Lovers*. Lydia insists that youth look to youth, and to its future living.
Ursula feels that she refreshes herself in the room which is 'a hushed
paradisal land'. Here, the living qualities of the great past come through
to her, in behaviour, attitudes, stories: they 'accumulated with mystic
significance, and became a sort of Bible'.

Ursula is aroused into sharp consciousness and response much earlier
than were Tom and Anna: she covers all the ground that they did, and
feels she has much farther to travel. So precociously exposed to adult
demands at home, she seizes at school all the means to keep widening the
circle of life. Like all Brangwen women, she sees education as the way to
the finer more vivid circles of life, adding her own note of dedication:
'She trembled like a postulant when she wrote the Greek alphabet for
the first time'. Even the fanciful, indifferent Gudrun recognises Ursula's
sense of mission: 'The younger girl lived her religious, responsible life
in her sister, by proxy'. There is in the older girl a fierce, fine compre-
hension, so that imaginative fancy is converted into self-exploration and
self-discovery. The novelist (ch. X, pp. 268–280) shows this self-
clarification in relation to 'the maximum day of the week', the Brangwens' Sunday. It represents a fine, even a beautiful, realisation of religion
in the English home. (It certainly correctively complements the more
famous depiction of the Clennams' Sunday in Dickens's *Little Dorritt*.)
Ursula's reflections and accommodations manifest her growth, her
refinement of sensibility, the verification of her purposive self. They also,
as repeatedly in her maturation, recreate spiritual stresses of her predecessors, and take these forward towards some resolution. Her history is
certainly individual, specific; nevertheless, its course increasingly reveals,
as climax to the careers of Tom, Will, and Anna, what form and issue
there is for 'the inner, impersonal great desires that are fulfilled in long
periods of time'.

The gladness, security, and the blessedness of the Brangwen Sunday
come from its distinctness: it expresses a religious sense separate from the
weekday sense. The sanctuary of Sabbath is its dedication to the eternal,

the immortal, the mystically transcendent. So Ursula relives Will's distaste for the ethical and evangelical, the surburban degrading of religious passion to a matter of 'What would Jesus do, if he were in my shoes?' She fights once more Will's battles with the pragmatic Anna, resenting her callous decrying of the 'dark, subject hankering to worship an unseen God'. The Lincoln Cathedral confrontation is all re-enacted, and the arguments about Christ the Lamb. Ursula's yearnings, dilating in romantic-sexual confusions of Launcelot and Jesus, harden into a substantial form: she seeks the image of the Sons of God. She contemplates the Old Testament reading in church—from *Genesis* 6, vv. 1–7—which recounts the legend of the Daughters of Men taken as wives by the Sons of God. She feels terror and compulsion, 'stirred as by a call from far off', as the vision takes hold of her of beings who 'had known no expulsion, no ignominy of the fall' (p. 274).

The symbolism of these prelapsarian figures crosses with the symbolism of the Flood as a mark of man's Fall. Retroactively, the Alfred Brangwen generation seem to be the last offspring of 'the unhistoried, unaccountable' legendary figures, heroic, angel-like. For Tom, in his speech at the wedding, a married couple together compose such a being. Anna sees Will in courtship as such a Son of God; again, 'dread flame of power', he appears to be 'the Angel of the Presence' (p. 167). It is in this realm of mythical, spiritual fullness of being that Ursula wishes to meet and to prove her lover, Anton Skrebensky. The legend of the Sons of God and the Daughters of Men crystallises all her desire for understanding, wisdom, and for the sexual and religious expression of her 'undiscovered self'. This image of a Son of God is the ultimate extension of adolescent yearnings centred first in Launcelot, then in a visionary Jesus. Its symbolic weight and spiritual substance can be gauged by a brief comparison with another novelist's use of the image:

> The truth was that Jay Gatsby of West Egg, Long Island, sprang from his Platonic conception of himself. He was a son of God—a phrase which, if it means anything, means just that—and he must be about His Father's business, the service of a vast, vulgar, and meretricious beauty. (*The Great Gatsby*, ch. VI)

F. Scott Fitzgerald only uses the allusion once, and briefly, where Lawrence uses it recurrently, and much more fully. Even so, the characteristic romantic irony gives the image acuteness in impact. It conveys with a sophisticated turn of expression the serious romanticism incarnated in Gatsby, and Fitzgerald's ambivalent fascination. By contrast, Lawrence's usage seems measured, deliberate, a degree pedantic.

Ursula's course of self-definition, outcome of her experiences in school and in church, is focused within the narrative's evocation of large-scale rhythms of living. This movement is the contrasting parallel to the realisation of the ancient rhythms: 'But heaven and earth was teeming around them, and how should this cease?' (p. 2). The Christian rhythms have supervened; and as in the Cathedral sequence, the novelist recreates from within the imminent, breathing sense of a way of life, and of how daily routine is permeated by a whole vision of life's meaning:

> The cycle of creation still wheeled in the Church year. After Christmas, the ecstasy slowly sank and changed. Sunday followed Sunday trailing a fine movement, a finely developed transformation over the heart of the family. . . . The chill crept in, silence came over the earth, and then all was darkness. . . . They moved quietly, a little wanness on the lips of the children, at Good Friday. . . . Then pale with a deathly scent, came the lilies of the resurrection, that shone coldly until the Comforter was given. . . .
> So the children lived the year of christianity, the epic of the soul of mankind. Year by year the inner, unknown drama went on in them . . . having at least this rhythm of eternity in a ragged, inconsequential life. (pp. 278–279)

Like its parallels in the narrative—the life of blood-intimacy, the rapture of the Cathedral—this evocation has genuine fidelity of perception. Yet the authenticity, in each case, goes with phrases, images, rhythms, which tease out a sense of what is questionable, fragile, likely to fail. So here, the lines on Good Friday, beyond their immediate aptness, are suggestive of a larger impoverishment of feeling, a diminution of dogmatic faith.

It is exactly around this crux of Christ's resurrection that her feelings undergo a great change. The sum of her reflections (closing ch. X) reads like an early form of the 1929 story, The Man Who Died. (A retelling in verse is The Risen Lord, C.P. I, p. 459.) Ursula's meditation, like the tale, is bold, original, and imaginatively persuasive. (None of the versions can be called blasphemous.) The redeeming power of love can only be experienced here and now; a gospel involving postponed salvation cannot be relevant to human needs. Wholly redemptive love must work in the flesh:

> The Resurrection is to life, not to death. Shall I not see those who have risen again walk here among men perfect in body and spirit, whole

and glad in the flesh, living in the flesh, loving in the flesh, begetting children in the flesh, arriving at last to wholeness, perfect without scar or blemish. . . . Is not this the period of manhood and of joy and fulfilment, after the Resurrection? (p. 280)

Resurrection becomes the type-figure in *The Rainbow* for awakening to life, the achievement of new selfhood by a relation that includes the extrapersonal, the connection with the cosmos witnessed in the sacrament of sexual passion. The narrative abounds in the proreptive imagery of germination and rebirth that advances to, then leads on from, this nodal symbolic centre. All these significations accrete around Ursula's chosen image, displacing the visionary spirit of Jesus, her image of the legendary Son of God, who will recognise her exceptionalness as a Daughter of Man.

Ursula seeks the unknown, the beyond, in her religious quest; simply she feels her father's church and faith have collapsed, are irrelevant now:

Passing the large church, Ursula must look in. . . . She had come to plunge in the utter gloom and peace for a moment, bringing all her yearning. . . . And she found the immemorial gloom full of bits of falling plaster, smelling of old lime, having scaffolding and rubbish heaped about, dust cloths over the altar. . . . The place echoed desolate. (p. 294)

The scene is an inverse mirror-sequence of Will's visit to the Cathedral; it echoes in a later scene, where the lovers visit Rouen Cathedral: 'She turned to it as if to something she had forgotten and wanted.' Its stability and its absoluteness, its unbrookable majesty can be seen in retrospect. But in the present, when Ursula first meets Skrebensky, the crumbling church signifies the end of an era. The catastrophe of the flood at Marsh Farm marked the death of the old way of life. This symbol of catastrophe marks the death of the succeeding mode, represented in Will Brangwen's life:

The place echoed desolate. . . . Skrebensky sat close to her. Everything seemed wonderful, if dreadful to her, the world tumbling into ruins, and she and he clambering unhurt, lawless over the face of it all. . . . (pp. 294–295)

Ursula's transvaluations serve the religious sense, they facilitate her life-quest. Her process of re-thinking Christian tenets, refashioning its images, re-assessing to significance, does certainly enact a representative career of an age's disillusionment. Yet its positives are not those of agnosticism or humanism: they are part of a delicate readjustment to the circumambient universe. They carry, as the last quotation suggests, some darker, near-demonic undertones. Forces hardly known to Tom and Lydia, which impinged upon Will and Anna's later relation, move nearer to the surface, to complicate and bewilder Ursula's struggle for fulfilment.

Ursula's reverence for life is not abated when the Church and its images crumble away. 'The magic land, where secrets were made known and desires fulfilled', far off on the horizon of early Brangwen women, can be surveyed as she walks from Cossethay:

> Ilkeston smoking blue and tender upon its hill, then her heart surged with far-off words: 'Oh Jerusalem, Jerusalem'. (p. 284)

She feels her task is making 'a transference of meaning from the vision world, to the matter-of-fact world'. (She loses the transforming imagination for a time, but recovers it in the final rainbow vision.) Forms, outlines, substance have to be created to release the religious ecstasy of which she feels strangely ashamed. The traditional moral imperatives have become as bogus and as desolate as the icons and the buildings. She sees only futility in turning the other cheek, or giving everything she has to the poor. It seems unclean and degrading to be humbly responsible to the world, to take on all burdens. Religion only fills her with sensuous yearning and sentimentality, which she detests. Ursula's questing spirit sees a hard, weekday value only in responsibility to oneself:

> How to act, that was the question? Whither to go, how to become oneself? One was not oneself, one was merely a half-stated question. How to become oneself, how to know the question and answer of oneself, when one was merely an unfixed something—nothing, blowing about like the winds of heaven, undefined, unstated. (p. 282)

The sudden appearance of Anton Skrebensky seems to promise an answer to Ursula's queries, a guide for her quest. Ursula responds to Skrebensky's aristocratic bearing, 'so distinct, self-contained, self-supporting'. (This echoes Tom's experience at Matlock, and also, hints at the relation of Anton to Paul Lensky, Lydia's first husband.) Being so young, Ursula is still tinged with romantic yearning: 'She laid hold of him at once for her dreams.' But these dreams have a substantial imaginative and visionary form, attested by the continuing Biblical allusions and symbolism: 'Here was one such as those Sons of God who saw the daughters of men, that they were fair.' Ursula reflects that Adam had made the human race a beggar, 'seeking its own being', and that this man is no son of Adam. The deeper inflections of the symbolism throughout this later narrative work to increase Ursula's dramatic stature. A sixteen-year-old schoolgirl is here represented as the fit agent to carry through a profound spiritual quest. The advent of Skrebensky is analogised as the renewal of God's covenant with the Chosen People (*Genesis*, 18):

> The house was changed. There had been a visit paid to the house. Once three angels stood in Abraham's doorway, and greeted him, and stayed and ate with him, leaving his household enriched for ever when they went. (p. 290)

The allusion to Abraham's enrichment is to his begetting a son and establishing his people. Skrebensky and Ursula share the enrichment of sexual passion: the force of the whole narrative action, with its poetic and mythic symbolism, represents this passion as sacramental.

Their first full encounter seems to achieve fulfilment of all the promised splendour. Its background is the very lively wedding-party of Fred Brangwen. The open air, the night-time, the haystacks, the play of light and shadow: all recall the sheaves-stacking scene of Will and Anna's courtship. There, deep called to deep, and the consummation was of the impersonal selves, a rich union. Their measured, varying rhythms of movement are echoed by Anton and Ursula's motions in dancing:

> They became one movement, one dual movement, dancing on the slippery grass. . . . It was a glaucous, intertwining, delicious flux and contest in flux. (p. 316)

Figures of light, glittering reflection, and fire for Ursula; figures of obscurity, shadow and darkness for Anton. This all promises the vital tension, the polarity of true, equal opposites, that will create union, not a passionate fusion. Aptly for the parallel of scenes, the presence of the moon attests a mysterious otherness, a suspension of the action in a realm of essential being. The moon is not the only spiritual presence: Anton registers apprehensively the presences of nature, 'the great new stacks of corn glistening and gleaming transfigured . . . themselves majestic and dimly present' (p. 319). Ursula sees them as 'something proud and royal, and quite impersonal', feeling that passion takes her to where they have their splendid being:

She turned with a great offering of herself to the night that glistened tremendous, a magnificent godly moon white and candid as a bridegroom, flowers silvery and transformed filling up the shadows. (p. 322)

In the polyphonic mode of this novel's poetic narrative, varied themes and 'subjects' can be counterpointed without violating dramatic order and logic. This sequence, with its mythic dimension, provides rich instances. Other forces and potentialities of the Anton–Ursula relation have been evoked along with the splendour of the positives—the moon, the natural presences, the sky, the dance, the fiery flux of passion. One counter-force comes from Ursula's uncle, Tom Brangwen, a cynical Bacchus who controls the wedding-feast, and who converts it with relish into a harvest-celebration, kindling in everyone a sensual release. Ursula shares the ecstatic delirium: 'It was as if a hound were straining on the leash, ready to hurl itself after a nameless quarry into the dark' (p. 316). The especial imagistic 'subject' associated with Tom, which becomes a controlling, comprehensive metaphor, is that of an oceanic underworld. Music and the darkness come in waves: 'One couple after another was washed and absorbed in the deep underwater of the dance' (p. 316). The duality, the dynamic concord, incarnated in the motions of the dance, is given a vitally different pitch and tone by this strategy of metaphor. By its means, the novelist creates a sense of the splendour and the strangeness, the beauty and the weirdness of human energies.

The symbolism becomes gravely insistent: 'They were both absorbed into a profound silence, into a deep fluid underwater energy that gave them unlimited strength'. This begins two short sections (pp. 316–317) evoking 'a vision of the depths of the underworld, under the great flood'. The movement recalls, reactivates the forceful symbolism of the flood that ended the early Brangwen era, and, in particular, the flood-imagery that dramatised the dangers, despairs, and terrors of Will and Anna's relationship. Even the predatory images are translated, and given this metaphoric tone. Ursula as an underwater creature feels a weight of dross that settles on her, sinks down with her 'cold, salt-burning body'. Skrebensky's urgency is to 'net her, capture her, hold her down . . . enclose her in a net of shadow, of darkness, so that she would be like a bright creature gleaming in a net of shadows, caught'.

There is failure in the passional relation of Anton and Ursula at this stage. Certainly the imagery of dissolution, water, cold brilliance, salt, is strikingly evocative of the anti-human and of the anti-organic. Yet the suggestion of Ursula's power and vitality, though inverted in its forms, gives pause to any simple assessment of this behaviour. Its very excessive-ness, its ultimacy of sensation, is paradoxically a positive: it launches Ursula on to the shores of the unknown, the terrible beyond. It is Skrebensky, in contrast, who follows a cult of the physical, because his desire is partial, it does not comprehend the totality of passion. His own earlier reflection hints at the inadequacy:

> Why could not he himself desire a woman so? Why did he never really want a woman, not with the whole of him: never loved, never worshipped, only just physically wanted her. (p. 315)

All Skrebensky's physical power and sexual attractiveness only serves to enforce the contrast: his fear of the unknown fills him with terror, makes him self-immolating: 'He knew he would die . . . he seemed to be clasp-ing a blade that hurt him. Yet he would clasp her, if it killed him' (p. 319).

It might seem either special pleading or absurd paradox to claim human worth and vitality in Ursula's behaviour in these phases of the action. A comparison with, say, a Thomas Hardy heroine—Sue Bride-head, for example—might be used to support a claim that the profoundest characterisation marks off aberration and perversity in conduct. The subtlety of such registration incorporates the centrally normal, human and psychological judgments. But to enforce such comparisons, by way of adverse assessment, is to misrepresent Lawrence's position and his responsibility to his insights into his times, and also to misrepresent his presented themes. A more just comparison would be with a Dostoievsky protagonist:

> As for me, all I did was carry to the limit what you haven't dared to push even halfway—taking your cowardice for reasonableness, thus making yourselves feel better. So I may turn out to be more *alive* than you in the end. Come on, have another look at it! Why, today we don't even know where real life is, what it is, or what it's called! . . . we don't know what to join, what to keep up with; what to love, what to hate, what to respect, what to despise! We even find it painful to be men—real men of flesh and blood, with our own private bodies; we're ashamed of it. . . . (*Notes from Underground*, Signet, p. 203)

As Eugene Goodheart suggests (in *The Cult of the Ego*), the underground man's exacerbated 'modern' sensibility endows him with value '*because* of the absence of the normal compromised qualities of men'. If Dostoiev-sky shows that this character has gone the whole way only in his mind,

Lawrence offers a version of such a representative sensibility that ventures to carry its own flesh and blood to the extremes of experience. Whatever their differences and contrasts, Ursula and the underground man are versions of Nietzsche's aristocrat, a figure whose fascination and para-doxical vitality come from a capacity to work through rejection to a more intense life: 'The aristocrat lives in an atmosphere of affirmation. He affirms himself: his negations simply enforce the distinction he makes between what is valuable (i.e. what he values) and what is not' (*The Cult of the Ego*, p. 100).

These references to parallels in the work of Dostoievsky and Nietzsche are offered as a shorthand summary of the kind and the direction of understanding implicit in the creation of an Ursula Brangwen. Though Hardy and George Eliot in a sense overlook the imaginative world of Marsh Farm, it is Dostoievsky and Nietzsche who preside over the realm in which the close of *The Rainbow* must be seen to have its tortured significations. Ursula is among the earliest of the many twentieth-century characters who are depicted as deliberate or instinctive immoral-ists—again, in a Nietzschean sense. These protagonists are shown as rejecting what he calls 'morality-in-itself'. Their creators implicitly and explicitly put by, as false or decadent morality, any idea of virtue which is unrelated to sharp recognition of the deep psychical needs of man, of 'what the heart really believes in' (*Fant.* p. 10).

Ursula is an immoralist, as Marvin Mudrick indicates, because there is no moral theorem that can take her through to the findings about life that she attains only through experience. She lives in the conditions out-lined by the underground man, unsure, with the collapse of sanctions and prohibitions, what to love or hate, what to respect or despise. Part of the desperation of her quest for life-values is in the choice of fulfilling the mastering impulses that shape her living at this time—with damage to herself and to those around and near her. She runs all the risks of her negations and egotistic affirmations, and marks herself as aristocratic, as more vitally propelled than a Winifred Inger or a Skrebensky. If fulfil-ment of her mastering impulses were possible, as Mudrick concludes, there at least might be a sane and a healing outcome. Ursula suffers in a world of breakdown, loss, and disrelation, and comes through to a world of possibility and of promise, if not yet of fulfilment.

The novelist has tried to represent, in Ursula's career, her spiritual quest for a form of passional living that would fulfil the individual by relationship, by satisfying the societal instinct. Her response to Skrebensky is potentially the means to make a Jerusalem out of an Ilkeston. The matter-of-fact world moulds Ursula's reflections and purposes. Quite early on, before the scene at the wedding, Ursula sharply probes Skrebensky's attitudes to soldiering, to war, to Empire, to patriotism. She asks what he would do without these preoccupations:

'Nothing. I would be in readiness for when I was needed.'
The answer came in exasperation.
'It seems to me', she answered, 'as if you weren't anybody—as if there weren't anybody there, where you are. Are you anybody, really? You seem like nothing to me.' (p. 309)

Here is one form of Anton's self-security, his certainty: he has whittled down his purposes to a few select principles. Since these are, in their isolation, social, public principles, he has stripped himself down to his social self. The insubstantiality of his 'soul's earnest purpose' is startlingly clear in the dialogue here. Unlike Will, he can never represent an archway, a door to the beyond; and this failure goes a long way to suggesting why Ursula is so corrosive to him in their encounters. In terms of her purpose, the failing even justifies her destructiveness.

Anton admits to himself his incapacity to feel total desire, to desire a woman with the whole of himself. His limitation to physical desire is not comparable to the absolute sensuality ascribed to Will Brangwen. Nor is there any causal connection alleged between this limitation of his sensual passion and the limitation of his outer self to its social form. (In none of the instances in the novel is there suggested a sexual inadequacy; it is a matter of the sensuality not incorporating principles beyond the physical.) For sexual and social expression are actions of the primal self, the under- or vital self; they are then symptomatic of soundness or of imperfection in that first, passional centre. This being so, the suggestion of perverse or displaced motive in Will's social activity is imaginatively, psychologically more apt than the neater, conventional motive that is offered.

A third and very interesting approach to these issues is represented by Tom Brangwen II. Where his brother Fred is another version of the first Tom, their father, this son is a sharp, fascinating study in contrast. He is educated, attractive, refined, and singularly different. He creates unease with his 'soft inscrutable nature, his strange repose, his informed air'. It takes the innocent eye of the young niece Ursula to see, along with the elegant demeanour, signs that he is 'bestial, almost corrupt'. She feels a thrill of revulsion, which attracts her nevertheless. Lydia senses the truth about her son: 'She could not but see the black depths of disintegration in his eyes, the sudden glance upon her, as if she could save him, as if he could reveal himself' (p. 250). Tom is Dionysian host, stimulating sensual release, at the harvest-wedding, licentiously prompting two beautiful women. He is prince of a dark, fluid underworld, creating strange splendour and perverse energies. The ecstasy of this flux, this dissolution, which fills Ursula with superb power, is undoubtedly an absolute. The glamour of Tom Brangwen is in distilling this ecstasy and power; his repulsiveness grows when he seems to turn against it, and so against himself:

> He too was at the end of his desires. He had done the things he had wanted to. They had all ended in a disintegrated lifelessness of soul, which he hid under an utterly tolerant good-humour. (p. 343)

Uncle Tom as colliery-manager at Wiggiston is totally conventional, charming, fine-mannered, because 'he had come to a stability of nullification'. He cares for nothing, man or woman, God or humanity. The marriage to Ursula's teacher, Winifred Inger, is part of this utter exhaustion of spirit. He comes to play the attentive husband and father, the model citizen, covering the ugly and spurious with sentimentality. (This seems to fill in the role Skrebensky will take as a married man.) Ursula brings the pair together, sensing a kinship in corruption. Winifred and Tom share a distaste for their own humanness, living in fear of relationship. They develop a perverse, 'ghoulish satisfaction' in witnessing the grotesque distortions of Wiggiston life. This modern mushroom version of Dickens's Coketown is not only mechanical, rigid, sterile; it is diseased, corrupt. It becomes an expression of the modern psyche, a city of unfulfilment, a symbol of what Tom and Winifred compulsively shape around them in their disintegration. It is the antipodal image to Ursula's vision of Ilkeston as Jerusalem.

That the geography here is psychic, spiritual, and Wiggiston a poetic symbol of the tendency of modern life, is a natural outcome of the narrative strategies of *The Rainbow*. It is underlined by the sexual metaphors that suggest Tom's predilections. In subjecting human bodies and lives to 'that symmetric monster' he attains 'a swooning, perverse satisfaction'. He jeers about the monstrousness of Wiggiston like 'a man who reviles his mistress, yet who is in love with her' (p. 349). Again, Tom and Winifred free themselves from self-hatred by abject servility to the machine.

D

Alongside this nullity and perversity, they yet have vestiges of strange power and energy. Their life is registered in images of the tropics, of sinister, lush vitality. In broiling sunshine, Tom

> had something marshy about him—the succulent moistness and turgidity, and the same brackish, nauseating effect of a marsh, where life and decaying are one. (p. 350)

On a very small scale, the kind of collocation being made, here and elsewhere in the book, is that of *Antony and Cleopatra*: decay and fruitfulness, fire and slime, corruption and natural growth. Lawrence's vision is of their interpenetration, their interinanimation, their vital complementarity. Wiggiston can thus, with this cosmic duality, undergo a rainbow change; Tom, Skrebensky, Will, though pulled towards disintegration, can embody splendid, strange energies.

There seems to be a peculiar form of the experience of religious conversion behind this aspect of the book's findings and values. Lawrence's concept of the unconscious, of the totality of selfhood, and of the primal, passional being is vital, central to his art in the novel. Religion, society, marriage, human relationships, all express the state of primal being. Imbalance, distortion or disease in these activities and relations signals impairment in the passional self, the vital sanity. All restoration to psychic, spiritual health is achieved at the living centre, or not at all. Any other 'reform' is external, a tinkering with the symptoms. Some scotch in the psyche, some check to the unfolding of the self, prevents the richest fulfilment of a Will Brangwen, a Skrebensky, a Tom. The rigidities or diseases of society then follow, mirroring the distortions of that society's representatives, leaders and participants. This seems to suggest that processes analogous to conversion can take place. There must be renewal at the passional core, and literally this is a life-choice. Failure to renew the self's purposive directions ends in the 'stability of nullification' ascribed to Tom. Clearly, the self has such choices for Lawrence, and is not the servant of a life-force. Though not defined in relation to conscience or moral duty, responsibility is central, and the agent answerable for his own most profound decisions.

Winifred Inger's career shows this failure of responsibility. A handsome, independent female, she first seems a model for Ursula's own development. She shows the girl how to discard the trappings of man's multiple forms of belief, to focus on the reality of the persisting aspiration within. Winifred's presence is like an enrichening sun, a nourishing warmth. Yet the first contact expressing their love is in water—a recapitulation of the symbolism of the wedding-dancing. Winifred in a Greek tunic has the pride and splendour of a Diana. At the river together, Ursula and Winifred inhabit 'an underworld of extinction, of oblivion'. Away from people, from light, from natural surroundings, Ursula comes to feel that the passion brings upon her 'a deep bottomless silence, darkness'. The older woman's 'fine intensity' becomes disintegrative, becomes clogging, dead, nauseous. Her manliness, her lesbianism, her feminism and materialism, all are indicative of the fear of herself and of relationships, expressive of the self-hatred that links her with Tom's pretences. She chooses to serve and to despise the machine, as she chooses spurious domesticity and social convention: it displaces self-hatred, contempt for self-nullification.

The graphic representation of Winifred and Tom follows the extended delineation, in Will and Anton, of the fearful struggle for release and fulfilment of man's shackled powers. Rich, incidental dramatic support is provided by scenes such as that with the impudent, gentle, richly responsive bargee (pp. 309–314); and others with the wary, intent, animal-like figures of the taxi-driver and the Sicilian waiter (pp. 469, 472–473). The series is continued in the presentation of the Brinsley Street school headmaster, Mr. Harby. Impressive, masculine, he strikes Ursula as a persistent, strong, but tethered creature. Occupied in a task too petty, like the other men, he yet brings himself to accept its servility, somewhat like Tom. He distorts his real being, violating his 'decent powerful rude soul'. The system he creates around him reflects this distortion: 'His system, which was his very life in school, the outcome of his bodily movement, was attacked and threatened at the point where Ursula was included' (p. 391). Conscious and so shameful of his own nullification, Harby builds up 'the fettered wickedness in him which would blaze out into evil rage in the long run'. The whole account of Ursula's school experiences is a detailed attestation of what is symbolised by the Wiggiston scenes. The ugliness, sterility, and the disease of a social system is a consequence of man's impoverishment. Harby, like Tom, cannot achieve 'a clear, pure purpose', must use his power and brute will, to project his inadequacy into grotesque forms outside himself. The school is a microcosm of the society; the character of Harby, like the many related figures, is not a study in neurosis, but a vivid, individual registration of the spiritual malaise of the time.

'Man's world of daily work and duty': Ursula has a compulsion to enter, to succeed there, to work from inside for change in Ilkeston and in Wiggiston. Yet so many forms of endeavour, like the struggle for female emancipation, strike her as a fight to get inside the cage, as a wish to be incorporated in a mechanical system. Winifred's militancy about science, education, and the vote went with a perversion of passion; Margaret Schofield's goes with a fibre-less romanticism:

> They talked of love and marriage, and the position of woman in marriage. Maggie said that love was the flower of life, and blossomed unexpectedly and without law, and must be plucked where it was found, and enjoyed for the brief hour of its duration. (p. 411)

Margaret might well come from the world of Arnold Bennett's *Anna of the Five Towns* (1902) or H. G. Wells' *Ann Veronica* (1909). Her conception of love is that enacted in Anna Tellwright's relation with Willie Price. Anna might even seem forerunner of Ursula in her quest:

> She dreamed impossibly of a high spirituality which should metamorphose all, change her life, lend glamour to the most pitiful surroundings, ennoble all the most ignominious burdens—spirituality never to be hers. (*A.F.T.*, pp. 74–75)

The anticlimax, the bathos of this last phrase is typical of the book which Lawrence scorned for its passivity and hopelessness. Ann Veronica seems more spirited in her scorn of a 'functionless existence varied by calls, tennis, selected novels, walks, and dusting in her father's house'. Yet her encounters with dissidents and suffragettes prompt Wells to facile satire: they are absurdly anti-male, faded, quaint, boring. Ann is shown concerned about love and marriage: her rebellion boils down to a few instances of very mildly anti-social behaviour. She sets up a home remarkably like her father's, and surprises her husband by a capacity for blind obedience.

For Wells' central affirmation in *Ann Veronica* does not concern love, women's position, or marriage. It springs from a vision of the power and joy of science. Ann is illuminated and enthralled as she realises it holds the key to life:

> It was the same Bios whose nature and drift and ways and methods and aspects engaged them all. And she, she in her own person too, was this eternal Bios, beginning again its recurrent journey to selection and multiplication and failure or survival. (*A.V.*, pp. 155–156)

Ann Veronica finds salvation in a philosophy of 'biologism', advocating immersion in vital life—as Lawrence and his characters are sometimes said to do. Ursula's vision of science, however, provides a very sharp contrast. At college, she chooses botany precisely because it shows 'something working entirely apart from the purpose of the human world'. She scorns what Ann and the scientist Capes would approve— the practical linking of college study and the demands of the industrial world outside. The Mount Pisgah to which education should lead turns out to be a coal-tip in an industrial wasteland:

> Always the crest of a hill gleaming ahead under heaven: and then, from the top of the hill only another sordid valley full of amorphous, squalid activity. (p. 436)

When Ursula turns like Ann Veronica to the contemplation of Bios, the source of her exhilaration is very different. She focuses her microscope on a slide of a plant-animal, and wonders about its nature and its purpose. She cannot absorb the professor's suggestion of impersonality, its neutral existence as a conjunction of forces—certainly not as a model of all life-forms. Unmechanical, it must be nodalised by a will, a purpose, a unifying self:

> Suddenly she had passed away into an intensely-gleaming light of knowledge . . . it was not limited mechanical energy, nor mere purpose of self-preservation and self-assertion. It was a consummation, a being infinite. Self was a oneness with the infinite. (p. 441)

'You may call the naked, unicellar bit of plasm the first individual, if you like . . . a specific individual, not a mathematical unit' (*P. & U.*, p. 209). It is precisely the individual's spontaneity and free play of self that is brutalised by the force of will, on both sides, in the mechanised systems of school and college, factory and mine. Ursula has felt the impossibility of offering love inside the systems, of rescuing matters by personal involvement. Love in such situations effects no more rescue than the vote or scientific knowledge. The saving vision for Ursula is of the irreducible, mysterious selfhood of the unicellar òrganism: 'To be oneself was a supreme, gleaming triumph of infinity.' In reviewing her life—'Already it was a history'—she feels, as her grandfather did, that so much experience has still left her essentially unformed. Firm in rejection, negative in action, her 'undiscovered self' is still unfolded:

> That which she was, positively, dark and unrevealed, it could not come forth. It was like a seed buried in dry ash. (p. 437)

For William Blake, the search for truth and fulfilment in the mundane world had to convert to seeking what that world considers demonic. This will prove to be the godlike, the divine. Ursula, renewing her quest by quitting the mundane world's lighted area, renews her vision of the dark angels. Skrebensky, heralded once as a Son of God, now returns: he brings the sense of rich darkness, changed by his years in Africa. 'She caught his brilliant, burnished glamour'. His male soul seems established, he has new livingness: their encounters enrich Ursula with 'living darkness'. She feels that her lover becomes 'her dark vital self'. Further, she seeks in sexual passion the sustaining touch of the unknown; it has in it some terror, but the challenge to Skrebensky is that they flood themselves with this 'rich fear'.

Yeats attributed to Lawrence a mythopoeic conception of life and art; *The Rainbow* certainly manifests this, especially in these final sequences. The staggering nature of Ursula's vision, which her passion with Skrebensky is to bring to realisation, to living form, is now revealed. Her quest is nothing less than the Blakean quest of the redemption of Albion. The extended sequence on the Sussex Downs (pp. 463–465) symbolises Ursula's desire for the rebirth of England, a spiritual renewal of everything and everyone. The central act is the sacramental act of sexual passion; its implications are unlimited, apocalyptic. The book opened with the image of the coupling of sky and earth: its reiteration now signifies the moment of regeneration:

> The high smooth downs . . . acknowledging only the heavens in their great, sun-glowing strength, and suffering only a few bushes to trespass on the intercourse between their great, unbateable body and the changeful body of the sky. (p. 463)

Ursula, like Birkin later, rolls naked on the ground, refreshing her spirit by a union with natural things. The love-making incarnates that of earth and sky, human and divine, a body-spirit union (p. 464). It converts all round to a perfection:

> Everything was newly washed into being, in a flood of new, golden creation. . . . It was so unutterably still and perfect with promise, the golden-lighted, distinct land. . . . (p. 465)

Ursula has dreamed like Adam, to awake and find it true. Skrebensky's role here is strange, but clear: he is part of Ursula's dream, a player in the rehearsal of her prophetic vision. The sexual union is symbolic, for Ursula mates with the sky and stars: 'It was not him (Skrebensky) . . . .

He was there, but only on sufferance. He was a screen for her fears. He served her' (p. 464). Once again, the emphasis is on the holy terror, the 'rich fear' of this union. Skrebensky trembles in apprehension, standing apart, 'overcome by a cruel ineffectuality', feeling that he is awaiting 'her judgment on him'. She is already forming that judgment:

> He seemed completed now. He aroused no fruitful fecundity in her. He seemed added up, finished. She knew him all round, not on any side did he lead into the unknown. (p. 473)

The sequence that includes the final love-making between Ursula and Skrebensky (pp. 476 ff.) is the reality, the total human enactment, for which the sequence on the Downs was a foreshadowing. The stars are replaced by the intense presence of the moon, witness of the haystack-scene:

> There was a great whiteness confronting her, the moon was incandescent as a round furnace door, out of which came the high blast of moonlight . . . a dazzling, terrifying glare. . . . (p. 478)

The allusion to Nebuchadrezzar's furnace (*Daniel*, 3) had symbolised Ursula's election as a witness of God (p. 193). Here, it both verifies that election, and identifies Skrebensky as one of the soldiers who were consumed, while the witnesses went unharmed. Walking by the sea, Ursula had been filled with the passion for fulfilment, yearning for the indifference, the strength, the 'salt bitter passion' it represents. But Skrebensky proves to be unequal to her need, no dark angel: 'His soul could not contain her in its waves of strength, nor his breast compel her in burning, salty passion' (p. 477). It is he who now sees her as a being of fearful potency: 'She was the darkness, the challenge, the horror'.

Anton was always attractive to her, and her feeling of fondness real; Ursula, though not only because she is pregnant, reacts against what she has done. She falls into acceptance of the way of life for which she scorned her mother. Restless, she walks through the October rain, for an hallucinatory encounter with the horses (pp. 486 ff.). Terror, power, and wonder combine in the abrupt, bewildering scene:

> Far back in our dark soul the horse prances. . . . And as a symbol he roams the dark underworld meadows of the soul. . . . The sons of God who came down and knew the daughters of men and begot the great Titans, they had 'the members of horses', says Enoch. (*Apoc.*, pp. 97–98)

In the relentlessness of her own earlier desires, refusing the passivity of the lamb, Ursula stretches her own limbs 'like a lion or a wild horse'.

Here, the action of the horses is in terms of gripping, pressing, clenching, bursting against restraint: 'But the darkness and wetness of rain could not put out the hard, urgent, massive fire that was locked within these flanks, never, never.' Ursula's compromise decision would, in effect, be such an attempt to put out the elemental fires within her (cf. *Fant.* p. 168). The immediate, particular application is clear: the spontaneous self would betray its own innermost vitality in accepting the nullity of conventional marriage with Skrebensky.

The setting of the scene indicates a wider, inclusive reference. The wooded shelter, an insistently enclosing circle, refers back to the enclosed life of the earlier generations. Ursula must make the disturbed, stormy crossing, 'back through all this fluctuation', to reach the highroad, the security of 'the ordered world of man'. Yet this pilgrimage can only be accomplished by full cognisance of the terrifying, wonderful creatures. They seem to come from some non-human realm, to symbolise more than man's own under-nature. They press in, press against 'the walls of time', like cosmic beings, or like the angelic sons of God. Their thunderous force must be acknowledged, not just by Ursula, but by the whole world of man. They embody, as Kinkead-Weekes points out, 'the eternal clash of opposites in all created things . . . an intensity of conflict that cannot be denied or reduced'. The imagery of fire and rain obliquely suggests the rainbow.

Ursula's rebirth, after the spiritual trauma of this encounter, is part of a reconciliation with the 'darker, older unknown'. The growth into the spontaneous self is suggested by one of the narrative's persistent images: 'The kernel was free and naked and striving to take new root, to create a new Knowledge of Eternity in the flux of Time' (p. 492). The false, conventional self passes away with the miscarriage of Anton's child. Salvation in the world of *The Rainbow*, however, is never singular. The rainbow-vision suggests that it is a reconciliation not only for Ursula, but for everyone. The amorphous, blackened town, the land of dry, brittle corruption, and the stiffened, coffined bodies, are all swept away, apocalyptically renewed:

And the rainbow stood on the earth. She knew that the sordid people who crept hard-scaled and separate on the face of the world's corruption were living still, and that the rainbow was arched in their blood and would quiver to light in their spirit, that they would cast off their horny covering of disintegration, that new, clean naked bodies would issue to a new germination, to a new growth. (p. 495)

Universal renewal has been implicit in the rainbow symbol throughout; so Will, on his marriage, feels that the surface of the world can be broken away entire, 'peeled away into unreality', leaving clear the reality inside (p. 146). The visions are prophetic, especially Ursula's, and not the signal for the rapture of an individual soul. Ursula's career in particular has been cast into a mythic dimension, so that her mission as prophet in the modern world has a dimension sustained in the terms of her ultimate visionary insights. A prophet is not a man of uncanny foresight, predicting the future with strange knowledgeability; but one with preternatural insight, awareness of what man is now, actually, potentially. Ursula's exemplary progress, her savage pilgrimage, gives her such profound awareness, and her experience authenticates the terms of her closing vision.

Ursula's quest contains that of all her predecessors; she has their knowledge and experience, though she must confront a different world. For the species of man, says Yeats, 'nothing so much matters as Unity of Being' (*The Trembling of the Veil*, Bk. V). This is exactly the distant rainbow that all the characters fix on instinctively. Yeats adds that Unity of Being can be sought, as by Goethe's Wilhelm Meister, 'intellectually, critically, and through a multitude of deliberately chosen experiences'. This, he says sharply, is treating human events as objects for a collector's cabinet. This aestheticising and intellectualising of consciousness that Yeats deplores also disturbed Lawrence. He also singles out the Goethe book, for its 'peculiar immorality', remarking that it discloses 'the perversity of intellectualised sex, and the utter incapacity for any *development* of contact with any other human being' (*L.II*, p. 1049). Yeats defines the quest for Unity of Being as the contrary to Wilhelm Meister's: 'True Unity of Being . . . is found emotionally, instinctively, by the rejection of all experience not of the right quality'. With Lawrence's comments, these contribute a definition of the form and purpose of Ursula Brangwen's quest. They help to indicate the major transvaluations Lawrence made in adapting the plot of education-by-experience that defines the traditional kind of *bildungsroman*.

The collector's-cabinet approach to experience means accumulating skills and values, storing up objects and events in an apprenticeship to a wise maturity. The material, the matter, even the quantity of experience is of prior value. Ursula Brangwen's approach, even though quantity, or, at least, range of experience counts, has its major stress on the manner of the quest. Urged to self-realisation, she tests the values of every area of activity and belief: family, education, love, church, society, nature. The values she finds active in each seem material ones to her, a question of matter and quantity: so many children, facts, or cattle, so many parts of a system. Ursula uses boundless energy not to acquire or attain a particular goal, but to strain towards what has not been attained. Like Tom Brangwen, like Will and Anna in their differing ways, Ursula seeks a stance that keeps alive her sense of the unknown. She cultivates the 'rich fear' of that sense, in all her relations and experience. Lawrence implicitly adopts, in his presentation of her turbulent 'modern' career, something akin to Kierkegaard's claim for the 'teleological suspension of morality'. Father Tiverton, pointing this out, finds that Lawrence consistently redefines morality in ways 'essentially religious, almost mystical'. He refers to this appropriate formulation:

> In his adventure of self-consciousness a man must come to the limits of himself and become aware of something beyond him . . . aware of that which surpasses him. . . . We have to be sufficiently conscious, and self-conscious, to know our own limits and to be aware of the greater urge within us and beyond us. (PX I, p. 185)

Ursula travels towards Blake's palace of wisdom, along the road of excess. Her rejections and destructiveness are not from any nihilistic passion. She means to acquire by struggle and suffering what cannot be simply imparted to her: 'The profoundest of all sensualities is the sense of truth'. There is no simple outside truth, to be contemplated and absorbed: it must be made to come alive inside the self. Ursula is Yeatsian man, who cannot know the truth, but can embody it.

One writer comments: 'Lawrence sees people's lives much as he saw history (and his letters reveal him as an ardent historicist), in terms of movements and tendencies, twilights and dawns, deaths and rebirths' (John Bayley, *The Characters of Love*, p. 29). Others have applied schemes, their own or Lawrence's, to this particular novel. Its tripartite structure seems to invite application of the three life-modes of the Hardy *Study*: the epoch of the Law, the epoch of Love, the advent of the Holy Spirit. (A movement then from Unity, through Differentiation, to their Reconcilement.) The *Study* discusses the Bible's threefold utterance: the declaration of God's approach (as with David); the rapture of the contact (as with Solomon); and the anguish of remembrance in separation (as with Job). This is adapted to the novel by Mark Kinkead-Weekes:

This is why the new novel had to have three stories or 'testaments': a beautiful but partial old world, in Old Testament style; a world of transition in which fulfilment is fused with failure, and the promised land is seen but not entered: a new world of maximum separation almost unto death, but retaining in extremity the memory of an abiding covenant.

Professor Kermode applies Kant's term, 'abderitist', to the novelist, since he explains history in terms of culture-cycles. He adds the further label, 'Joachite', one who postulates three historical epochs, one for each person of the Trinity, with related notions of transition and crisis.

The historian who takes the world's corruption to herald catastrophe and dissolution is called a 'moral terrorist' by Kant. The description is transferred by Kermode to Lawrence, stressing as he does that persistence in decadence, rottenness, in the 'last wave of time' are part of the strange joy before total disintegration and renewal:

> You ask me about the message of *The Rainbow*. I don't know myself what it is: except that the older world is done for, toppling on top of us.... There must be a new world. (*L.I*, p. 422)

This comment must be taken alongside the later remark about *Women in Love*: 'It is purely destructive, not like *The Rainbow*, destructive-consummating.' The war gives a dark tinge to his comments, and affects the tone of the later novel intensely—though not, as he explains, the tone of *The Rainbow* (*L.I*, p. 519). Elsewhere, as corrective, he can be found describing how man is 'eager always to make new worlds, out of this old world, to bud new green tips on the tree of life'. Each tip springs from the apparent death of the preceding world: but it is a great collapse rather than death: 'It must carry through all the collapse the living clue to the next civilization' (*Fant.*, pp. 176–177):

> I do not believe in evolution, but in the strangeness and rainbow-change of ever-renewed creative civilizations. . . . Nothing will ever quench humanity and the human potentiality to evolve something magnificent out of a renewed chaos. (*Fant.*, p. 8)

Later in the discussion, Lawrence defines three life-modes: that of tradition (instance, China); that of idealism (instance, Europe); and that of impulse (instance, the South Seas). All are authentic modes, but no one must exist alone, or in dominance. The distinctions could be illustrated from the successive generations, and from their recapitulation in Ursula's own development (her relations with Schofield and Skrebensky

illustrating the modes of tradition and impulse respectively, and her responses to the church, the mode of idealism). What is fairly obvious is that
the stages of the action, whether labelled historically, Biblically, or philo-
sophically, are also elements in the development of the individual. The
emphasis falls on how larger movements, in history and society, are the
outcome or the expression of human activity. Inside all the metaphorical
abstractions, historical or ideological categories—part of what Lawrence
called 'pollyanalytics'—is this stress on the human and on the individual.
The resilience of humanity, the human potentiality for renewal and
creation from chaos, is there in the way Ursula emerges from her
exposure to devastating experiences. Like Tom Brangwen, like young
Anna Lensky, Ursula is a character fashioned from concern, care, the
perceptiveness of love.

The narrative that contains these authentically imagined and lovingly
perceived figures has none of the intellectually patterned march deplored
in Goethe's work, and none of the abstract design suggested by many of
the three-part categories. Much of the continuity catches the forms of
life's ongoingness—place, home, familial atmosphere. Development and
change spring from the beautifully rendered play of connections between
parent and child. John Bayley alleges that Lawrence's larger patterns
move towards metaphorical abstraction, adding: 'The continuity of
The Old Wives' Tale gives much more impression of what people actually feel their lives to be like.' In so far as this means the daily outsides of
our living, and an acute sense of time's passing, this is fair. Bennett's
perceptions, as E. M. Forster remarks, make us feel 'Of course'—con-
cluding that a great book, however, must rest on more than being
'strong, sincere, sad' (*Aspects of the Novel*, pp. 38–39). The something
more in *The Rainbow* can be suggested, for example, in the dimensions
of Tom Brangwen's portrayal. He embodies a life-truth, without
breaking the mould of his ordinariness. The spectrum of a figure like
Tom goes from the carbon of his character through to his sense of
relation to the cosmos. His ordinariness and his dramatised uniqueness
defy generality, and give warrant to our sense that this is what people can
actually feel their lives to be like. Life according to a Constance Baines,
in *The Old Wives' Tale*, is too drastically a matter of 'Of course'. What a
Tom Brangwen adds, by way of credible complexity, is thought:

> Thought is a welling-up of unknown life into consciousness. . . .
> Thought is a gazing on to the face of life, and reading what can be
> read.

Thought is pondering over experience, and coming to conclusion. . . .
Thought is a man in his wholeness wholly attending. (*C.P.* II, p. 673)

The Rainbow dramatises 'thought' in this comprehensive sense as it
manifests itself in various generations and in a wide range of characters.
Man's relation to the cosmos, his religious being, is established and re-
established in the urgent quests of each central figure. Ursula, however
extraordinary, however singularly 'modern', is seeking what Tom
sought, driven by the need that defines their common humanity:

This is our need, our imperative need. It is a need of the mind and soul,
body, spirit and sex: all . . . a renewal for ever of the complete rhythm
of life and death, the rhythm of the sun's year, the body's year of a
lifetime, and the greater year of the stars, the soul's immortality. . . .
We *must* get back into relation, vivid and nourishing relation to the
cosmos and the universe. The way is through daily ritual and the re-
awakening. . . . Vitally, the human race is dying. It is like a great
uprooted tree, with its roots in the air. We must plant ourselves again
in the universe. (*PX* II, p. 510)

Sharp self-criticism and the capacity to re-work so painstakingly—
here, up to seven times for this novel (*L.I*, p. 264)—gave Lawrence the
confidence to assess the work objectively. 'I am sure of this now, this
novel. It is a big and beautiful work' (*L.I*, p. 272). By late April 1914, the
work no longer 'missed being itself'. Retitled at Frieda's suggestion,
The Rainbow had now to be defended against Garnett's derogatory
remarks, the artist stressing his work's newness and profound seriousness:

All the time, underneath, there is something deep evolving itself out
in me. And it is *hard* to express a new thing, in sincerity. . . . But
primarily I am a passionately religious man, and my novels must be
written from the depth of my religious experience . . . you should see
the religious, earnest, suffering man in me first. (*L.I*, p. 273)

The kind of defence Lawrence makes is indicative of the kind of work
he had attained. The themes he shares with Wells, Galsworthy, and
Bennett—changes in society, the emancipation of women—serve all the
more sharply to focus the difference. The topical and popular subjects are
utterly transformed, so that Lawrence's novel seems to have little or no
relation to the range of works with which it was to compete. Something
happens that is akin to Richardson's taking over the form of the story-
in-letters, or to Jane Austen's adoption of the story of courtship and

marriage. One facet of the originality of *The Rainbow* is manifested in what source the novelist traced his action back to: Tom Brangwen's career. A good novelist might well have dramatically counterposed the parents' relationship to the girl's own relationships; and even singled out the independent, assertive spirit of Anna, the mother. It took completely original novelistic planning to represent Tom's development, and his marriage to a foreign widow. That the account begins with the male's search for fulfilment in a new mode of life gives unexpected breadth and depth to the total movement. The liberation of woman becomes one kind, or even becomes the type of the richly human struggle for identity, relation, fulfilment with others, and fulfilment in relation with the life of the cosmos.

The Rainbow underwent a trial-by-reviewers in October 1915. In mid-November, the examining magistrate at Bow Street ordered the seizure and destruction of all copies. In early November 1915, in a letter to Edward Marsh, editor and litterateur, Lawrence wrote: 'You rather jeered at *The Rainbow*, but notwithstanding, it is a big book, and one of the important novels in the language. I tell you, who know.' He told Lady Cynthia Asquith that Marsh's opinions were impertinent, if not insulting: 'It's a true novel, and a big one.' The tone of the writer's comments is not shrill or querulous—rather, it is one of firmness, and, in the circumstances, one of courage. Where Marsh jeered, John Galsworthy, 'very calmly and *ex cathedra*', announced to its author that the novel was 'a failure as a work of art'. Such attitudes and pronouncements, as Lawrence remarked, damaged the giver as well as the receiver. For surely, about this achievement, the writer was correct: he had composed a big book, which is one of the important novels in the English language. The bigness is not simply in its scale and in its range, its *Middlemarch*-like panorama of life in the provinces. Its considerableness grows from its raising triumphantly from that wide social action—a defining quality of the traditional English novel—certain forms of other actions. These are dramatic qualities and rhythms that prompt the definition which Lawrence would welcome for *The Rainbow*: a religious novel. It consequently belongs to a small, select number of such works, and raises itself from a regional English context into a fully European one.

Select Bibliography

Colin Clarke, *River of Dissolution: D. H. Lawrence and English Romantic-ism.* Routledge & Kegan Paul, 1969

Colin Clarke, editor, *D. H. Lawrence: The Rainbow and Women in Love.* Macmillan Casebook, 1969: especially 'Lawrence and the Apocalyptic Types', Frank Kermode (pp. 203–18); 'The Narrative Technique of *The Rainbow*', Roger Sale (pp. 104–16)

Peter Coveney, *The Image of Childhood.* Peregrine, 1967: on Lawrence, pp. 320–336

H. M. Daleski, *The Forked Flame.* Faber & Faber, 1965

George Ford, *Double Measure.* Holt, Rinehart & Winston, 1965

Alan Friedman, *The Turn of the Novel.* O.U.P., 1966: on Lawrence, ch. 6, pp. 130–178

Eugene Goodheart, *The Utopian Vision of D. H. Lawrence.* University of Chicago, 1963

Arnold Kettle, *An Introduction to the English Novel*, II. Grey Arrow, 1962: on *The Rainbow*, pp. 115–140

Mark Kinkead-Weekes, 'The Marble and the Statue: The Exploratory Imagination of D. H. Lawrence', in *Imagined Worlds*, edited M. Mack and I. Gregor. Methuen: pp. 371–418

Laurence Lerner, *The Truthtellers: Jane Austen, George Eliot, D. H. Lawrence.* Chatto, 1967

Harry T. Moore, *The Life and Work of D. H. Lawrence.* Unwin, 1963

Julian Moynahan, *The Deed of Life.* Princeton University, 1963

Marvin Mudrick, 'The Originality of *The Rainbow*', in *A D. H. Lawrence Miscellany*, edited Harry T. Moore. Heinemann, 1961

J. I. M. Stewart, *Eight Modern Writers.* Clarendon Press, 1963

Father William Tiverton (pseud. Martin Jarrett-Kerr), *D. H. Lawrence and Human Existence.* Rockliff, 1951

William Walsh, 'Ursula in *The Rainbow*', in *The Use of the Imagination.* Chatto, 1959, pp. 163–74

Virginia Woolf, 'Notes on D. H. Lawrence', in *Collected Essays*, I. Hogarth Press, 1968

Index